The Huey Long Murder Case

By Hermann B. Deutsch

The Huey Long Murder Case

The Huey Long
Murder Case

by Hermann B. Deutsch

Doubleday & Company, Inc.
Garden City, New York, 1963

In Boundless Affection, This Modest Volume
Is Dedicated to
THE LYING NEWSPAPERS
A Generic Term Applied by Huey P. Long to
The Free Press of a Free Republic.
Especially is it dedicated to any and all who
during almost half a century have been
My Fellow Workers
As Typified by
John F. Tims and Ralph Nicholson
And Most Specially Is It Dedicated to the Memory of
Richard Finnegan and Marshall Ballard.

Contents

FOREWORD

Until I undertook to gather all available evidence for what I hoped to make a definitive inquiry into the circumstances of Huey Long's assassination, I had no idea of how many gaps there were in my knowledge of what took place. Yet except for the actual shooting, which fewer than a dozen persons were present to see, and for what then took place in the operating room of Our Lady of the Lake Sanitarium, most of what had any bearing on the circumstances took place before my eyes.

Consequently I am so deeply indebted to so many who were good enough to fill those gaps with eyewitness reports, that no words of mine could begin to settle the score. Chief among those whose claims on my gratitude I can never wholly acquit are Dr. Cecil A. Lorio of Baton Rouge, one of the only two surviving physicians who played any part in the pre-operative, operative, and post-operative treatment of the dying Senator; Dr. Chester Williams, the present coroner of East Baton Rouge parish, who made it possible for me to see, study and understand the microfilmed hospital chart sketchily covering the thirty hours that elapsed between the time of the shooting and its fatal termination; Col. Murphy J. Roden, retired head of the Louisiana State police, who was the only person to grapple with Dr. Weiss; my friend and for many years colleague, Charles E. Frampton; Sheriff Elliott Coleman of Tensas parish; Chief Justice John B. Fournet of the Supreme Court of Louisiana; and Juvenile Court Judge James O'Connor, who carried the stricken Kingfish to the hospital after the shooting.

No less am I under obligations to Earle J. Christenberry,

Seymour Weiss, and Richard W. Leche, to whom I owe so much of the information on background elements that alone make intelligible some of the otherwise enigmatic phases of what actually occupied no more than a fractional moment of crisis.

My thanks are likewise tendered to Captain Theophile Landry, formerly an officer of the state police; to General Louis Guerre who was that organization's first commandant; to Adjutant-General Raymond Fleming of Louisiana; to Charles L. Bennett, managing Editor of the Oklahoma City *Times*; and particularly to Dr. James D. Rives and Dr. Frank Loria of New Orleans.

To my one time professional competitor but always close friend, Congressman F. Edw. Hebert, I tender this inadequate word of appreciation for the assistance so freely rendered by him in gathering material. To another friend and colleague, Charles L. Dufour, I am deeply indebted for assistance in proofreading.

And finally, I am more grateful than I can say to my brother Eberhard, an unfaltering—and what is more, successful—champion before the courts of the principle of press freedom, for advice in preparing the final draft of this manuscript; to LeBaron Barker for invaluable suggestions in revising the original draft; and to all others who, in ways great and small, have been of assistance in making possible the completion of this task.

Hermann B. Deutsch.

Metairie, La.
October 31, 1962

The Huey Long Murder Case

> *"Assassination has never changed the history of the world."*
>
> ———DISRAELI

The motives which prompt a killer to do away with a public figure are frequently anything but clear. On the other hand, the identity of such an assassin rarely is in doubt. The assassin himself sees to that, in obvious eagerness to attain recognition as the central figure of a world-shaking event.

President McKinley, for example, was shot down in full view of the throng that moved forward to shake his hand at the Pan-American Exposition in Buffalo. Czolgosz, his anarchist assassin, boasted of his deed, making no effort to escape. John Wilkes Booth, one cog in a large plot, did not withdraw in the dimness of the stage box from which he fired on Lincoln, but leaped into the footlights' full blaze to posture and declaim: *"Sic semper tyrannis!"*

In recent times the perpetrator of an unsuccessful attempt at mass assassination actually clamored for recognition. When the late Cardinal Mundelein became archbishop of Chicago in 1919, community leaders tendered him a banquet of welcome. At the very opening of the repast, during the soup course, the diners became violently ill. By great good fortune—probably because so much poison had been introduced into the soup that even the first few spoonfuls caused illness before a fatal dose could be taken into the system—

none of the diners lost his life as a result of the decision of
an assistant cook, Jean Crones, to do away with the leaders of
Catholicism in Chicago.

The cook made good his escape. He has never been ap-
prehended. But for days he sent a letter each morning to the
newspapers and to the police telling just how he had kneaded
arsenic into the dumplings he had been assigned to prepare
for the soup, how he had later bleached his hair with lime
whose fumes almost overcame him, in just which suburbs he
had hidden out on which days, and so on. Short of surrender-
ing to the police, he did all that lay in his power to identify
himself as one who had attempted a mass murder of un-
precedented proportions.

One could go down a long list of political assassinations
throughout the world during the past century, and find that
almost without exception the identity of the extroverted killer
was not a matter of the slightest doubt. No one questions
the fact that a Nazi named Planetta murdered Engelbert
Dollfuss in his chancellery, that Gavrilo Prinzip shot the
Archduke Francis Ferdinand in Sarajevo, or that President
Castillo Armas of Guatemala was killed by a Communist
among his bodyguards, Romero Vasquez, who underscored
his part of the plot by committing suicide.

In modern history, however, one political assassination is
still being hotly debated, not merely as to the motives which
prompted the deed, but as to the identity of the one whose
bullet inflicted the fatal wound. This was the killing of Huey
P. Long, self-proclaimed "Kingfish" of Louisiana, who was
on the very threshold of a bold attempt to extend his domin-
ion to the limits of the United States via the White House
when Dr. Carl Austin Weiss, Jr., fired on him, and was almost instantly mowed down by a fusillade from the weapons
of the bodyguards with whom Senator Long surrounded himself wherever he went.

To this day, nearly thirty years after the event, there are those who believe that the assassination was part of a plot of which President Franklin Roosevelt had cognizance and in which representatives of his political organization participated. Only a month prior to his death Huey Long had charged publicly on the Senate floor that, at a secret conference in a New Orleans hotel, representatives of "Roosevelt the Little" had assured the other conferees the President would undoubtedly "pardon the man who killed Long."

There are those who accept the coroner's verdict that the homicidal bullet was fired by young Dr. Weiss from the eight-dollar Belgian automatic pistol he had purchased years earlier in France where he was doing postgraduate work in medicine. According to his father, testifying at the inquest which followed the deaths of the two principals, Dr. Weiss carried this pistol in his car at night, ever since intruders had been found loitering about the Weiss garage.

A great many others—quite possibly a majority of those who express an opinion on the matter—insist that the bullet of whose effects Long died was not the one fired by Dr. Weiss, but a ricochet from one of the bodyguards' guns in the furious volley that followed.

Still others, and among these are many of the physicians and nurses who knew Dr. Weiss well, feel certain to this day that he did not fire a shot at all, that he was not the sort of person who could have brought himself to take the life of another human being. It is their contention that Dr. Weiss merely threatened to strike the Kingfish with his fist—may indeed have done so, since Long did reach the hospital with an abrasion of the lip after he was rushed from the capitol to Our Lady of the Lake Sanitarium. After the blow or threat of one the young physician was immediately gunned down, according to this version of the incident, a chance shot thus inflicting the wound of which, some thirty hours later, Senator Long died.

The foregoing contradictory views are still further complicated by the fact that there are many with whom it is an article of faith that regardless of who fired the ultimately fatal shot, the leader they idolized would have been saved but for an emergency operation performed on him that same night by Dr. Arthur Vidrine.

Finally, there is no agreement to this day on what could have prompted Dr. Weiss to commit an act which almost everyone who knew him still regards as utterly foreign to his nature. No valid motive for this deed has ever been definitively established. One assumption has it that the doctor was the chosen instrument of the "murder conference" whose discussions Long made the text of the last speech he delivered on the Senate floor.

Others feel that inasmuch as Long was on the point of gerrymandering Mrs. Weiss's father, Judge Ben Pavy, out of the place on the bench he had held for seven successive terms, Dr. Weiss's act was one of reprisal. At least one connection of the Weiss and Pavy families has held that Dr. Weiss was actuated purely by a patriotic conviction that only through the death of Long could his authoritarian regime be demolished and liberty be restored to Louisiana.

In view of the foregoing, one question poses itself rather relentlessly: At this late date is an effort to compose such far-ranging differences of conviction and surmise worth while? Can any purpose beyond a remotely academic recording of facts be served thereby? Is there anything that distinguishes in historical significance the assassination of Huey Long from the public shooting which in time brought about the death of, let us say, Mayor William Gaynor of New York?

It is because those questions seemed to answer themselves, and unanimously, in the affirmative that the data chronicled in the following narrative were gathered. They represent among other items the statements of every surviving eyewitness to the actual shooting, and of surviving physicians who were present during, or assisted in, the emergency operation performed by Dr. Vidrine. They include the never previously revealed hospital chart of the thirty hours Senator Long was a patient at Our Lady of the Lake Sanitarium.

This was no easy search for truth. There are still those who refuse to discuss the assassination of Huey Long with anyone who does not share to the fullest their individual views of what took place. None the less, the significance of two figures—Franklin Roosevelt and Huey Long—so curiously alike and yet so dissimilar, indicated a genuine need to weigh every scrap of obtainable evidence and assess any rational conclusions to be drawn from them.

During the early 1930s no two names were better known in the United States than those of Roosevelt and Long. The former was the product of a patrician heritage plus the gloss of Groton and Harvard. The latter had received no formal education beyond that afforded by the Winnfield high school. An intermittent career as a book auctioneer, Cottolene salesman, and door-to-door canvasser in the rural South did nothing to soften the rough edges of his early environment. No two modes of address could have differed more radically than the polished modulation of F.D.R.'s fireside chats and the bucolic idiom of one of Huey Long's campaign rodomontades: "Glory be, we brought 'em up to the lick-log that time" —"He thinks he's running for the Senate but watch us clean his plow for him come November"—"Every time I think of how I was suckered in on that proposition I feel like I'd ought to be bored for the hollow horn."

It was once stated that before Seymour Weiss, the New Orleans hotel man who was perhaps his closest friend, took him in hand, he dressed like a misprint in a tailored-by-mail

catalogue. The description was apt. Early photographs prove
it, if proof be needed. Even when he was oil-rich from his
expanding law practice in Shreveport, he wore a ring in which
a huge diamond gleamed, and a tie-pin in which another,
equally large, was set.

"Stop talkin' po'-mouth to me, son," an elderly legislator at
Baton Rouge once advised him. "You got di'monds all over
you. Bet you even got di'mond buttons on yo' draw's."

None the less he was superbly endowed with what, for
want of a better term, might be called personal magnetism,
a quality that drew crowds as sheep are drawn to a salt trough.
Nowhere was this manifested more strikingly than in Washington, where throngs packed the Senate galleries the moment it was known that he was about to deliver a speech.

He was a superb actor, too. Telling the same anecdote
seven or eight times a day, day after day in campaign after
campaign, he would none the less deliver it with the same
chuckling verve at the thousandth repetition with which he
had told it initially. Little bubbles of laughter escaped him
as though involuntarily when he built up to the nub of a
jest. The effect of such tricks of stagecraft was heightened by
the unhurried but uninterrupted flow of words, the affectation
of homely idiom, the Southerner's easy slurring of consonants.

In Arkansas, at the time of the unparalleled Caraway campaign of 1932, every gathering set a new attendance record
for the time and place. The address Long delivered from the
band shell at Little Rock drew the largest crowd ever assembled in the history of the state. And when the motorized
campaign party whipped from one city to the next to meet
the demands of a tightly co-ordinated speaking schedule,
crowds lined even the back roads through which the cars
passed; crowds of those who, unable for one reason or another to leave their small farmsteads in that depression-
harried autumn, waited patiently by the dusty roadsides for

a fleeting glimpse of the limousine in which Huey Long whizzed by them.

He was at his best in the rough and tumble of partisan politics, both on the hustings and on the Senate floor. When Harold Ickes said Huey had "halitosis of the intellect," Long retorted by dubbing him "the chinch bug of Chicago." To be sure, this was after he had broken with the Roosevelt administration, when, scoffing at the Civilian Conservation Corps, he offered to "eat every pine seedling they'll ever grow in Louisiana." At the same time, when arguing fiscal policy with the Senate's veteran on such matters, Carter Glass, he said bluntly in the course of debate that "I happen to know more about branch banking than the gentleman from Virginia does."

In these respects, as in matters of politesse, Roosevelt was the very antithesis of the gentleman from Louisiana. Yet neither would brook opposition from within his partisans' ranks. The breach between Roosevelt and as selfless a supporter as James A. Farley was to all intents and purposes identical with the disagreements that broke the ententes between Long and every campaign manager and newspaper publisher who had ever supported his candidacy. Escaping conviction on impeachment charges, he announced: "I'll have to grow me a new crop of legislators in Louisiana." When some of Roosevelt's early New Deal legislation was nullified by the Supreme Court, the President promptly sponsored a bill to increase the number of Supreme Court justices, with himself to name at one swoop six additional members; and he did his best to force what was widely referred to as his "court packing" measure through Congress.

Long campaigned vigorously through the Dakotas, Minnesota, Nebraska, and other northern Midwest states for Roosevelt in 1932. Some of these states went Democratic for the first time in more than a generation. Admittedly this was not all due to Long's stump speeches. But no one knew better than Franklin Roosevelt that much of his success in the Long-toured regions was due to the gentleman from Winnfield. He was one of the few political leaders who did not under-estimate the Long potential, who correctly evaluated the Long influence in overturning the politics of Arkansas to make Hat-tie Caraway the first woman ever elected to a full term in the United States Senate. He had few illusions, if any, on the score of the national organization of personal followers Long was building through his Share-Our-Wealth clubs.

Under the circumstances it was inevitable that these two, neither of whom would ever admit a potential palace rival into the inner circle of his aides, should become implacable opponents. Long was on the point of announcing his candi-dacy for president against Roosevelt for the 1936 campaign when a bullet cut short his career. The challenge he proposed to fling at the man who subsequently carried all but two of the Union's states was neither a forlorn token like that of Governor Landon, nor a visionary crusade like the campaign of Henry Wallace and Glen Taylor. No one appraised this more realistically than Roosevelt himself. He never under-estimated the sort of monolithic organization Long could create around the hard core of existing Share-Our-Wealth clubs, the amount of whose mail, as delivered to the Senate office building, dwarfed that delivered to any other member of the Congress.

In pursuance of his objective, Earle Christenberry, with Raymond Daniell of the New York *Times*, had completed, by midsummer of 1935, the manuscript of a short book to be signed by Huey Long, under the title of *My First Days in the White House*. He had written no part of this rather naïve treatise himself, though he had discussed it in general terms with those who did draft it. An earlier book "by Huey P. Long"—*Every Man a King*—was actually a collaboration in which the prophet of Share-Our-Wealth had dictated sections to the late John Klorer, then editor of Long's weekly *American Progress* (née *Louisiana Progress*), who later became a successful scenarist in Hollywood. But the helter-skelter discussions in which Long outlined his ideas for *My First Days in the White House* were turned into reasonably coherent prose by Daniell and Christenberry; much of the manuscript Long never even saw until it was in final form.

It was an artless bit of oversimplified future history, written in the past tense to describe the inauguration of President Huey Long, his appointment of a cabinet (Herbert Hoover, Franklin Roosevelt, and Alfred E. Smith were among its members), and the adoption of national Share-Our-Wealth legislation under the supervision of a committee headed by John D. Rockefeller, Jr., and Andrew W. Mellon! But it was gauged for an audience which already believed that it was possible to redistribute all large fortunes among the nation's have-nots. It was never meant to convert economists, financiers, and magnates. On the contrary, its principal purpose was to notify all and sundry, especially "all," that Huey Long was a candidate for president and was confident of victory.

During that early autumn of 1935 the United States stood at a windy corner of world history. In Europe totalitarians had taken over Italy's tottering liberal monarchy in 1922, and in 1933 the "republic" of Germany. In Louisiana a home-grown fascist with complete dominance over his own state was challenging the national leadership. Long had already put into operation at the local level an authoritarian principle of governmental sovereignty. Legislative and judicial functions were almost wholly concentrated in the hands of an executive who was in reality a "ruler." The architect of that change was setting himself to expand it to national dimensions.

The seriousness of this situation was recognized by observ-

ers of the national scene. Raymond Gram Swing listed five
public figures in a volume entitled *Forerunners of American
Fascism* and named Huey Long as the one of potentially
greatest national danger. The others were Fr. Coughlin, William Randolph Hearst, Sr., Theodore G. Bilbo of Mississippi,
and Dr. Townsend. George Horace Lorimer, long-time editor
of the *Saturday Evening Post,* ordered a three-part serial pro-
file of the senator from Louisiana. Most of this was published posthumously, as was all of what was to have been
Long's *Mein Kampf: My First Days in the White House.*

Kingfish was thus tapped for a vaulting effort to become
America's *Duce* or *Führer* when violence put an abrupt end
to the design and to the life of its protagonist. Official records in the coroner's office at Baton Rouge give no details
beyond those embodied on a printed form, whose blank spaces
were filled in to note the name, age, bodily measurements,
color, and sex of the decedent, together with a curt nota-
tion ascribing death to a "gunshot wound (homicidal)."

Nearly thirty years have passed since those notations were
entered on an official form to be filed in the archives of East
Baton Rouge parish. Death has by now claimed many of the
witnesses whose testimony might have been of value in de-
termining what actually took place in the marble-walled corridor where the Kingfish, hurrying along with characteristically
flapping stride, received his mortal wound. But many other
presential witnesses yet survive.

No inquest worthy of the name has ever been conducted
to decide and record officially what the circumstances of Huey
Long's assassination were. The family refused to authorize a
necropsy. The death of Dr. Vidrine in 1955 was a portent of
the rapid and inevitable approach of the day when the last
eyewitness would have passed on. No one would then be
able to relate at first hand any detail of the violent moment
which averted a conflict pitting the two best-known public

figures in the United States against one another for virtual sovereignty over this nation.

That violent moment would thus pass into history as a confused welter of mutually contradictory versions, of rumors, half truths, and whole untruths. Amid these the Huey Long murder case would remain an unsolved and probably insoluble mystery. It was for this reason that I undertook several years ago to gather and collate whatever eyewitness testimony might still be available. I had known Senator Long and his family for many years. Of the newsmen who heard Huey Long make his first state-wide political address at Hot Well on July 4, 1919, I am the only one still actively reporting the course of events and the doings of public figures. I had accompanied him not only on any number of his state campaigns, but also on the remarkable Caraway campaign of 1932.

I knew nearly all of his intimates, and was on first-name terms with most of them then in the easy camaraderie of journalism. Without exception every surviving witness I approached has given me his version of what took place in the capitol corridor at the time of the shooting. With but one exception every witness who was present in the operating room and in the sickroom where Huey later died, has told me all that he saw, heard, or did on that occasion.

These several accounts do not agree at every point. Indeed, here and there they are rather widely at variance. For that very reason they merit belief. Such differences validate the integrity of testimony so given. Had these accounts tallied in every minute particular after the passage of more than a quarter of a century, or even after the passage of twenty-five minutes, they would have been suspect, and properly so. It is axiomatic that eyewitness accounts of the same event invariably differ, even when given at once. The classic illustration of this is the prize fight at whose conclusion one judge awards the victory to Boxer A, the referee calls the combat a draw, and the other judge selects Boxer B as the winner.

The fact that there is no variance whatever between accounts given by several witnesses, especially when their testimony concerns an occurrence involving violence, is as certain an indication of collusive fraud as is the fact that two signatures, ostensibly penned by the same individual, show not the slightest difference in form, shading, or pen pressure at any point. Unless one or both such signatures are forgeries, absolute identity is a practical impossibility.

The question of whether or not the Kingfish could have wrested political control of the United States from Franklin Roosevelt became academic when a bullet found its mark in his body. But a glance at the highlights of his career offers some of the clues to what happened to him on September 8, 1935.

> *"The iniquity of oblivion*
> *blindly scattereth her poppy,*
> *and deals with the memory of*
> *men without distinction to*
> *merit of perpetuity."*
>
> ——SIR THOMAS BROWNE

One day some of the VIP's of the Long political hierarchy were gathered in the office of Governor Oscar Allen when a matter of legislative procedure was under discussion. It is worth noting for the record that the Governor's chair was occupied by Senator Huey Long. Governor Allen sat at one side of his desk. The names of the others do not matter. Among them were highway commissioners, a state purchasing agent, floor leaders from House and Senate, the head of an upstate levee board, and the like.

Huey was issuing orders and lost his temper over the apparent inattention of some conferees, who were conducting a low-voiced conversation in a corner of the room.

"Shut up, damn it!" he shouted suddenly. "Shut up and listen to me. This is the Kingfish of the Lodge talking!"

From that day on he was "Kingfish." Even Franklin Roosevelt, telephoning him from New York during the hectic maneuvering which preceded that summer's Democratic national convention, greeted him with the words: "Hello, Kingfish!"

The self-proclaimed Kingfish was named Huey Pierce Long

at his birth on August 30, 1893, the third of four sons born to Huey Pierce Long, Sr., and Caledonia Tyson Long. The family farm was near Winnfield, and by the standards of that place and time the Longs were well off; not wealthy, to be sure, but never in want. Winnfield, seat of Winn parish, is a small wholly rural community not far from the center of the state.

"Just *near* the center of the state?" Westbrook Pegler once asked Senator Long incredulously after watching him put his legislative trained seals through their paces. "Just *near* the center of the state? I'm surprised you haven't had the legislature declare it to *be* the center of the state."

Scholastically, Huey did not distinguish himself, and he took no part in athletics, lacking the physical pugnacity that is the heritage of most young males. His brother Earl, two years younger than Huey, frequently asserted that "I had to do all Huey's fighting for him." But as long as he remained in high school (he left after a disagreement with the principal and before graduation) he was the best debater that institution ever numbered among its pupils.

His first essay into the realm of self-support came at age fourteen, when he loaded a rented buggy with books and drove about the countryside selling these at public auction. In doing so he laid the foundation for what became the largest personal acquaintance any one individual ever had among the farm folk of Louisiana.

"I'd never stay at a hotel, even later on, when I was out selling Cottolene or baking powder or lamp chimneys or whatever," he would boast. "I always drove out beyond town to a farmhouse where they'd take me in and put up my horse, and I would pay them something and put in the evening talking to them, and later I would make it my business to drop those folks a post card so they'd be sure to remember me."

At summer's end he entered Oklahoma University at Norman, hoping to work his way through law school as weekend drummer for the Kaye Dawson wholesale grocery. That did not work out. After a heated disagreement with the head of the business he returned to Louisiana and became a door-to-door salesman for Cottolene. In glorifying this product he held cake-baking contests here, there, and yonder.

"My job was to convince those women they could fry chickens, steaks, or fish in something else besides hog lard, and bake a cake using something else besides cow butter," he explained. "I would quote the Bible to them where it said not to use any part of the flesh of swine, and if I couldn't convince them out of the Bible, I would go into the kitchen and bake a cake for them myself."

First prize for one of his cake-baking contests in Shreveport was awarded to pretty Rose McConnell. Not long thereafter, she and Huey were married. With all his savings and a substantial loan from his older brother Julius, he managed to finance nearly a year of special study at Tulane University's law school in New Orleans. He and Rose shared a room in a private home not far from the university, where among other furnishings, a rented typewriter was installed.

Young Mr. Long would bring home a law book, drive through it in furious haste while his phenomenally retentive memory seized every really salient detail, "and then I would abstract the hell out of it, dictating to my wife, who would type it out for me." With barely enough money for housing, carfare, short rations, and such essentials as paper and pencils, it is none the less probable that these were the least troubled, most nearly contented and carefree days the couple would ever know. Before year's end he was admitted to the bar, and returned to Winnfield with Rose to begin practice.

He soon realized that despite local successes, the ambitious goals he had set for himself could be attained only in a much larger field. So he moved to Shreveport, which was just at the threshold of a tremendous boom following the discovery of oil in the nearby Pine Island areas. By accepting royalty shares and acreage allotments for legal services in examining titles and the like, Huey was on the threshold of becoming very wealthy, when he and the other Pine Islanders discovered that they could not send their black gold to market unless they sold it at ruinously low prices to owners of the only available pipeline. Long's implacable hostility toward the Standard Oil Company had its inception then and there.

As first step in a campaign to have pipelines declared common carriers, he became a candidate for the Railroad (now Public Service) Commission and was elected. The brothers Long presented a solid front on this occasion, Julius and Earl working like beavers to help Huey win. George ("Shan") had moved to Oklahoma by that time to practice dentistry. Only once thereafter were they politically united, and that was when Huey ran for governor in 1928.

Commissioner Long made his first state-wide stump speech the following year at a rally and picnic which six candidates for governor had been called to address. He had not been invited to speak, but asked permission to say a few words—and stole the show!

One must picture him: a young man whose bizarre garb was accented by the fact that since he was wearing a bow tie, the gleaming stickpin with its big diamond sparkled from the otherwise bare band of his shirt front. The unruly forelock of rusty brown hair, a fleshy, cleft chin, and a general air of earnest fury all radiated anger. His blistering denunciation of the then governor as a pliant tool of the Standard Oil Company, and his attack on the state fire marshal, an anti-Long politico from Winnfield, as "the official barfly of the state of Louisiana" captured all the next day's headlines.

Thenceforth the pattern of his future was set. He continued his attacks on trusts and large corporations, certain that this would enlarge his image as defender and champion of the downtrodden "pore folks." His assaults became so intemperate that in 1921, Governor John M. Parker filed an affidavit against him with the Baton Rouge district attorney, and thus brought about his arrest and trial on charges of criminal libel.

His attorneys were his brother Julius, Judge James G. Palmer of Shreveport, and Judge Robert R. Reid of Amite. He was found guilty, but his reputation as a pitiless opponent was already so great that only a token sentence was imposed: one hour's detention, which he served in the Judge's chambers, and a one-dollar fine. He was so delighted by the outcome that he gave his youngest son, born that day, the names of his attorneys: Palmer Reid Long. Also, some years later, he saw to it that the judge who had imposed the token penalties was elected to the state supreme court.

Continuing his onslaughts against millionaires and monopolies, he ran for governor in 1924 on a platform of taxing the owners of great fortunes to aid the underprivileged in their struggle for a reasonable share of the better life: education for their children, medical care for all who could not afford to pay, and some sort of economic security for all who toiled, be it in factory, market place, mine, or farm.

He now inveighed against Wall Street as a whole, not merely against isolated corporations as before. The Mellon fortune and the House of Morgan came in for their oratorical lumps; but it is a matter of record that later, when Earl and Huey had fallen out, the former testified under oath before a Senate investigating committee that he had seen his brother accept $10,000 from an official of the Electric Bond and Share Company "in bills so new they looked like they'd just come off the press."

However, from every stump Huey proclaimed that "ninety per cent of this nation's wealth is in the hands of ten per

cent of its people. . . . The Bible tells us that unless we redistribute the wealth of a country amongst all of the people
every so often, that country's going to smash; but we got too
many folks running things in Louisiana and in Washington
that think they're smarter than the Bible."

None the less he ran third in a three-man first primary. In
view of the fact that he had no organized backing it must
be conceded that it was a close third, an amazing achievement
the credit for which must be given to his wide acquaintance
among the farm population and the matchless fire of his
eloquence. A number of factors contributed to his defeat.
One of them undeniably was his refusal, or inability, to recognize that he "could not hold his liquor." After a convivial
evening at a lake-front resort in New Orleans, he drove back
to town with his campaign manager at a wildly illicit speed
and was promptly halted by a motorcycle officer. His campaign manager hastily explained to the patrolman that the
car was his, and that his chauffeur, one Harold Swan, had
merely acted under orders. But the fact that Huey Long and
Harold Swan in this instance were one and the same came
out later, along with accounts of how Huey had gone tipsily
from table to table at the Moulin Rouge inviting all and
sundry to be his personal guests at his inaugural ball.

Ordinarily, this might have won him votes in tolerant
south Louisiana, where prohibition was regarded as the fig-
ment of sick imaginations, like the *loup garou*. But in south
Louisiana he had few backers in that campaign to begin with,
being a north Louisiana hillman; and in north Louisiana,
where drinking had to be done in secret even before the Vol-
stead Act became nominally the law of the land, such reports
were sheer poison.

Finally, the weather on election day turned foul. The
wretched dirt roads of the hinterlands where Huey's voting
strength was concentrated became impassable, so that many

of his supporters could not reach their polling places. But four years later, when he once more ran for governor in yet another three-man race, he barely missed a majority in the first primary. No run-off was held, however, because one of his opponents announced he would throw his support to Long, pulling with him many followers, including a young St. Landry parish physician, Dr. F. Octave Pavy, who had run for lieutenant governor. Under the circumstances a second primary would have been merely an empty gesture of defiance.

As governor, he rode roughshod over all opposition to his proposal to furnish free textbooks to every school child, not merely in the public schools, but in the Catholic parochial schools and the posh private academies as well; for a highway-improvement program which he proposed to finance out of increased gasoline taxes. Nor was he one to hide his light under a bushel in pretended modesty. On the contrary, after each success he rang the changes on Jack Horner's classic "What a good [in the sense of great] boy am I." Moreover, it made little difference to his devotees whether his promises of still greater benefits for the future, or boasts about the wonders he had already achieved, were based on fact or fiction.

By way of illustration: Dr. Arthur Vidrine, a back-country physician, was catapulted into the superintendency of the state's huge Charity Hospital at New Orleans, and later was additionally made dean of the new state university College of Medicine Long decided to found. Vidrine had won the new governor's warm regard by captaining the Long cause in Ville Platte, where he was a general practitioner.

In some quarters there is a disposition to regard Arthur Vidrine as no more than a hack who relied on political manipulation to secure professional advancement. While it is obvious that his original support of, and later complete subservience to, Huey Long brought him extraordinary preferment, it must not be overlooked that in 1920, when he was graduated from Tulane University's college of medicine, he was a sufficiently brilliant student to be chosen in open, nonpolitical competition for the award of a Rhodes scholarship, and that for two years he took advantage of this grant to pursue his studies abroad.

After his return he served for a time as junior intern at New Orleans' huge Charity Hospital . . . and within four years he was made superintendent of that famous institution and dean of his state university's new medical school, both appointments being conferred on him by newly elected Governor Huey Long, who lost no opportunity to picture his protégé as something of a miracle man in the realm of healing.

To an early joint session of the legislature, His Excellency announced that under his administration Dr. Vidrine had reduced cancer mortality at Charity Hospital by one third. This was obvious nonsense. Had it not been, the medical world would long since have beaten a path to the ornamental iron gates of the century-old hospital in quest of further enlightenment.

One of the newspapers finally solved the mystery of this miracle of healing. It stemmed solely from a change in the system of tabulating mortality statistics. Calculated on the old basis, the death rate was precisely what it had been before, a little better in some years, a little worse in others. All this was set forth publicly in clear, simple wording. But except for a few of the palace guard, who cynically shrugged the explanation aside, not one of the Long followers accorded it the slightest heed. They and their peerless standard bearer continued to glory in the "fact" that he had reduced Charity's cancer death rate by a third.

This accomplishment was by no means the only one of

which young Governor Long boasted. Less tactfully, and certainly less judiciously, he made vainglorious public statements to the effect that "I hold all fifty-two cards at Baton Rouge, and shuffle and deal them as I please"; also that he had bought this legislator or that, "like you'd buy a sack of potatoes to be delivered at your gate."

Within a year the House of Representatives impeached him on nine counts. Huey had learned that such a movement was to be launched at a special session in late March of 1929, and sent word to his legislative legions to adjourn *sine die* before an impeachment resolution could be introduced. But an electric malfunction in the voting machine made it appear that the House voted almost unanimously to adjourn, when in fact opinion was sharply divided. A riot ensued, which was finally quelled when Representative Mason Spencer of Tallulah, a brawny giant, bellowed the words: "In the name of sanity and common sense!" Momentarily this stilled the tumult and Spencer, not an official of the House, but merely one of its members, called the roll himself, by voice, on which tally only seven of the hundred members voted to adjourn.

The committee of impeachment managers in the House was headed by Spencer and by his close friend, another huge man, George Perrault of Opelousas. However, the impeachment charges were aborted in the Senate, when Long induced fifteen members of that thirty-nine-man body to sign a round robin to the effect that on technical grounds they would refuse to convict regardless of evidence. Since this was one vote more than enough to block the two-thirds majority needed for conviction, the impeachment charges were dropped.

Spencer and Perrault remained inseparable friends, occupying adjacent seats in the House to the day of Perrault's death during the winter of 1934. On the night of September 8, 1935, Huey stopped to chat momentarily with Spencer, who took occasion to protest against the appointment of Edward Loeb, who had replaced his friend Perrault.

"All these years I've got used to having a man the size of George Perrault sitting next to me," he complained. "Did you have to make Oscar appoint a pint-size member like Eddie Loeb to sit in his place here?"

"You remind me," retorted Long, "of the old nigger woman that was in a bind of some sort, and her boss helped her out, giving her clothes or money or vittles or whatever. So she said to him: 'Mist' Pete, you got a white face, fo' true, but you's so good you's bound to have a black heart.' That's you, Mason. Your face is white, but you've sure enough got a black heart."

A year after the abortive impeachment Long announced he would run for the Senate forthwith, though his gubernatorial tenure would not be terminated for another two years. In this way, he said, he would submit his case to the people. If they elected him, they would thereby express approval of his program. If not, they would elect his opponent, the long-time incumbent senator. Long was elected overwhelmingly, and then went from one political success to another, electing another Winnfieldian, his boyhood chum Oscar Allen, to succeed him as governor, and smashingly defeating a ticket on which his brother Earl was running for lieutenant governor with his brother Julius' active support. It was later that year that Earl testified against Huey before a Senate committee.

In that same year Huey Long entered Arkansas politics. Mrs. Hattie Caraway, widow of Senator Thad Caraway, had been appointed to serve the few remaining months of her husband's term, then announced as a candidate for re-election. Huey had two reasons for espousing her candidacy. First, she had voted with him for a resolution favoring the limitation of individual incomes by law to a maximum of a million dollars a year. Secondly, the senior senator from Arkansas, Majority Leader Joe T. Robinson, who had turned thumbs down on this resolution, had endorsed one of the candidates opposing Mrs. Caraway's election. Thirdly, he felt it was time to put the country on notice that Kingfishing could be carried successfully beyond the borders of its home state.

Mrs. Caraway was accorded no chance to win. Every organized political group in the state had endorsed one or another of her six opponents, among whom were included a national commander of the American Legion, two former governors, a Supreme Court justice, and other bigwigs. The opening address of the nine-day campaign Huey Long waged with Mrs. Caraway was delivered at Magnolia, just north of the Louisiana border. At its close, a dazed local political Pooh-Bah wired a major campaign headquarters in Little Rock: "A tornado just passed through here. Very few trees left standing, and even those are badly scarred up."

It was here that Long first formulated what later became the Share-Our-Wealth clubs' credo.

"In this country," he proclaimed, "we raise so much food there'd be plenty for all if we never slaughtered another hog or harvested another bushel of grain for the next two years, and yet people are going hungry. We've got enough material for clothes if in the next two years we never tanned another hide or raised another lock of cotton, and yet people are going barefoot and naked. Enough houses in this land are standing empty to put a roof over every head at night, and yet people are wandering the highways for lack of shelter."

The remedy he proposed was simple: share our wealth instead of leaving almost all of it in the hands of a greedy few.

"All in this living world you've got to do," he insisted, "is to limit individual incomes to one million dollars a year, and fix it so nobody when he dies can leave to any one child more than five million dollars. And let me tell you something: holding one of those birds down to a measly million dollars a year's no sort of hardship on him. At that rate of income, if he stopped to bathe and shave, he'd be just about five hundred dollars the richer by the time he got his clothes back on.

"What we got to do is break up those enormous fortunes like the billion-dollar Mellon estate. By allowing them a million dollars a year for spending-money you'll agree we wouldn't be hurting 'em any to speak of. We'd have the balance to distribute amongst all the people, and that would fix things so everybody'd be able to live like he could right now if he made five thousand a year. Yes sir, like he was having five thousand a year and a team of mules to work with, once we share the wealth!"

Today it is almost impossible to visualize the effect of so alluring a prospect on a countryside forced at that time to rely on the Red Cross for seed corn and sweet-potato slips to assure a winter's food supply. The rural Negroes in particular, their "furnish" sadly shrunken as a result of the depression, accepted it almost as gospel that Huey Long was promising them five thousand dollars a year and a team of mules.

The impact of Long's oratory was so clearly obvious that a special committee waited on him at Texarkana, where he planned to close the campaign on Saturday night, to ask that he remain in Arkansas over the weekend to address meetings in the tier of counties along the Mississippi River on Monday, the day before the election. He agreed to do this, canceled plans to drive to Shreveport from Texarkana, and drove back to Little Rock instead. Since this left the accompanying newsmen with no grist for the early Monday editions, and since he had been quoting the Bible right and left in his speeches, not to mention the fact that in the glove compartment of his Cadillac a well-thumbed Bible reposed beside a loaded revolver and an atomizer of throat spray, he was asked where he expected to attend church the next morning.

"Me go to church?" he inquired incredulously. "Why I haven't been to a church in so many years I don't know when."

"But you're always quoting the Bible and so . . ."

"Bible's the greatest book ever written," he interrupted, "but I sure don't need anybody I can buy for six bits and a chew of tobacco to explain it to me. When I need preachers I buy 'em cheap."

Mrs. Caraway's first primary victory was a landslide. Well pleased, Huey returned to Louisiana to defeat two-term incumbent Senator Edwin S. Broussard and elect one of his chief attorneys in the impeachment case, John H. Overton, in his stead. It was this election which a Senate committee later investigated to sift allegations of fraud. The investigation was recessed midway to give Senator Long an opportunity to halt a threatened bank run by the simple expedient of having Oscar Allen proclaim Saturday, February 4, a holiday celebrating the fact that sixteen years before, on February 3 and 4, 1917, Woodrow Wilson had severed diplomatic relations with Germany!

PROCLAMATION
STATE OF LOUISIANA
EXECUTIVE DEPARTMENT
BATON ROUGE

Whereas, on the nights of February 3 and 4, 1917, Woodrow Wilson, president of the United States, severed diplomatic relations with the Imperial German government; and

Whereas, more than 16 years has intervened before the

great American people have turned their eyes back to the lofty ideals of human uplift and new freedom as propounded by Woodrow Wilson; and

Whereas, it is now fitting that due recognition be given by the great State of Louisiana in line with the far-reaching principles enunciated by the illustrious southerner who sought to break the fetters of mankind throughout the world;

Now, therefore, I, Oscar Kelly Allen, governor of the State of Louisiana, do hereby ordain that Saturday, the fourth day of February, 1933, the 16th anniversary of the severance of diplomatic relations between the United States and the Imperial German government be, and the same is hereby declared, a holiday throughout the State of Louisiana and I do hereby order that all public business, including schools, colleges, banks and other public enterprises be suspended on said day and that the proper ceremonies to commemorate that event be held.

In witness whereof I have caused to be affixed the great seal of the State of Louisiana on this, the third day of February, in the year of Our Lord, A. D. 1933.

Oscar Kelly Allen
Governor

Attest:

E. H. Conway
Secretary of State.

This meant that all public offices, schools—and banks— were legally forbidden to open their doors on that Saturday; by Sunday the Federal Reserve authorities had put $20,000,-

ooo at the disposal of the menaced bank and the run which might have spread panic throughout the country died a-borning. However, bank closures on a national scale were thus postponed for only a month. March 4, while Franklin Roosevelt was taking his first oath as president, state after state was ordering its banks to close, as financial consternation (vectored from Detroit, however, and not from New Orleans) stampeded across the land.

One of the newly inaugurated President's first acts—"The only thing we have to fear is fear itself!"—was to order all the nation's banks to close until individually authorized by executive permit to reopen. But the onus of having initiated the disaster had been averted from Louisiana by Huey's bizarre bank holiday, and this underscored the fact that for some time past, the number and ratio of bank failures in Louisiana had been far, far below the national average. It also strengthened the growing conviction that Louisiana's Long was something more than another Southern demagogue like Mississippi's Bilbo or Texas' Pa Ferguson.

Franklin Roosevelt was probably never under any illusions on that score. He gauged quite correctly the omen of Share-Our-Wealth's growing strength. It had been blueprinted for all to see when Mrs. Caraway's candidacy swept the boards in Arkansas, and again when this movement, plus the oratorical spell cast by the Louisianian in stumping the Midwestern prairie states, carried them for Roosevelt later that same autumn. According to Long's subsequent diatribes, he had campaigned thus for "Roosevelt the Little" on the express understanding that the president-to-be would back the program for limiting individual incomes and bequests by statute.

There is ample ground for the belief that Long was secretly gratified when he realized that the New Dealers would have none of this proposal. The issue which had served him so well in the past could thus be turned against Roosevelt four years later, when Long planned to enter the lists as a rival candidate for the world's loftiest office. Publicly, to be sure, he professed himself outraged by "this double cross," bolted the administration ranks once more, repeated an earlier, defiant fulmination to the effect that if the New Dealers wished to withhold control over Louisiana's federal appointments from him, they could take this patronage and "go slap dab to hell with it."

Roosevelt and his *fidus Achates*, Harry Hopkins, took him at his word, and gave the anti-Long faction, headed by Mayor Walmsley of New Orleans, a controlling voice in the distribution of federal patronage. The breach between the two standard bearers—one heading the New Deal and a federal bureaucracy tremendously swollen by a swarm of new alphabetical agencies, the other all but worshiped as archangel of Share-Our-Wealth—widened from month to month.

Roosevelt left the anti-Long philippics to members of his cabinet and other department heads: Hugh Johnson, NRA administrator, for example, or Interior Secretary Harold Ickes. The climax to these interchanges came in the late summer of 1935, when in an address delivered on the Senate floor, Long charged that "Franklin Delano Roosevelt the first, the last, and the littlest" was linked to a plot against his—Huey Long's—life.

> *"I haven't the slightest doubt*
> *but that Roosevelt would par-*
> *don anyone who killed Long."*
> ——UNIDENTIFIED VOICE FROM
> A DICTOGRAPH RECORD QUOTED
> BY HUEY LONG IN AN ADDRESS
> BEFORE THE UNITED STATES
> SENATE

Long's charge that he had been selected for assassination by a cabal in whose plot President Roosevelt was involved at least by implication made headlines from coast to coast and filled page on page of the *Congressional Record*. But it fell quite flat, being taken in a Pickwickian rather than in any literal sense. Even the unthinking elders of the Share-Our-Wealth clubs, their numbers now sadly shrunken by reason of the march of time, still cling to a rather pathetic belief in this extravagant bombast only by reason of an uncanny and unrelated coincidence: within less than thirty days after making the charge Long actually was assassinated.

His climactic thrust at the White House was not taken too seriously at the time, however, because, for one thing, Long had cried "plot against me" too often. By the fall of 1935 the story was old hat, even though it had never before been blazoned in so august a tribunal as the Senate, and had never before involved, even by indirection, a chief executive. On two previous occasions he had placed Baton Rouge under martial law, calling out the militia, to defend him against plots on his life. Only seven months before making the Senate speech in question he had "exposed" the plot of a group of Baton Rouge citizens, a number of high officials among them, to waylay his automobile on a given night while he was being driven to New Orleans, and kill him at a lonely bend of the River Road where the car would of necessity have to slow down.

In proof of this he put on the witness stand an informer who had infiltrated into the ranks of the supposedly plotting group, and who testified as to the details of a conspiracy.

Early in his senatorial career he had made himself so offensive in the washroom of a club at Sands Point, Long Island, that the irate victim of a demand to "make way for the Kingfish" slugged him. Since the blow split the skin over an eyebrow, the incident could not be concealed. Long promptly charged that hired bravos of the House of Morgan had assaulted him in the club washroom, intent on taking his life.

Finally, when what he told the Senate on that August day in 1935 was boiled down in its own juices it made pretty thin gruel, as anyone who cares to wade through the fine print of the *Congressional Record* for that date can see for himself. The truth is that on the eve of Congress' adjournment, Long was trying to build up against Roosevelt something he could tub-thump before the voters in the next year's presidential campaign.

On the principle that "the best defense is an attack," he was keeping the New Deal hierarchy in Washington so busily occupied on another front that he could take advantage of their preoccupation to infiltrate Louisiana's federal patronage with his followers.

Presumably control over these appointments to all sorts of oddball positions under the PWA, WPA, and other auspices was now in the hands of the anti-Long contingent, headed by among others a good half of the state's members in the lower house of Congress. But these were parochial politicians, fumblingly inept at organizing such matters on a state-wide scale. To cite but a single example, one project sponsored under the anti-Long dispensation was a review of the newspaper files in the New Orleans City Hall archives. By direction of Mayor Walmsley, so many appointees were packed into this particular task that they had to work in one-hour-a-day shifts in order to find physical room in the small garret-like space set aside for it.

Theoretically, they were to index these files, and to repair torn pages with gummed tape as they came across them. Actually, they would for the most part merely turn the leaves of the clumsy bound volumes until they came to the Sunday comics or other such features, and read these at leisure. Then they repaired to Lafayette Square when their hour of demanded presence was up, and joked about the way they would put out of joint the noses of the anti-Long leadership on election day; for of course most of them were dedicated Share-Our-Wealthers eagerly looking forward to $5000-a-year incomes when Huey Long got around to redistributing the nation's wealth.

Meanwhile their Kingfish was giving the anti-Long leaders a real Roland—an entire battalion of Rolands, in fact—for their patronage Oliver. The spoils-system theory of a patronage plum is that its bestowal is good for three votes; in other words, that the recipient and at least two members of his family or circle of friends will vote for the party favored by the job's bestower. A United States senator would normally be consulted about appointments to all federal patronage posts not covered by civil service in his state: Collector of the Port, Surveyor of the Port, Collector of Internal Revenue, district attorneys, federal judges, and the like. During the early New Deal era this roster was tremendously amplified by the staffs of numerous new alphabetical agencies and their labor force.

Huey Long may not have expected to be taken quite so literally when he told the Roosevelt hierarchs they could take their patronage "slap-dab to hell" as far as he was concerned. But when he saw that he was indeed given no voice in any Louisiana federal appointment, he initiated an entire series of special sessions of the state legislature which subserviently enacted a succession of so-called "dictatorship laws." Under these statutes he took the control of every parochial and municipal position in every city, village, and parish out of the hands of the local authorities, and vested the appointive power in himself.

He did this by creating new state boards, composed of officials of his own selection, without whose certification no local public employee could receive or hold any post on the public payroll. A board of teacher certification was thus set up and without its—which is to say, Huey Long's—approval, no teacher, janitor, school-bus driver, or principal could be employed by any local parish or city school board. No municipal police officer or deputy sheriff throughout the state, no deputy clerk or stenographer in any courthouse, no city or parish sanitary inspector, and so on down the entire line of public payroll places, could continue in his or her position unless specifically okayed by Senator Long. In those pre-civil-service days the appointive state, parish, and city employees in Louisiana outnumbered the federal patronage places within the state by hundreds to one, even during the New Deal's era of production controls and "recovery."

Hence, for each federal patronage job he had nominally lost to his opponents he gained hundreds—literally—of local appointments which were thenceforth at his disposal. When this was pointed out in the anti-Long press and he was asked for comment, he chuckled and said: "I'm always ready to give anybody a biscuit for a barrel of flour."

In sum, he had brought practically all local public employees, including those who staffed Mayor Walmsley's city administration in New Orleans, under the Long banner by the summer of 1935. Only a scant handful of "dictatorship laws" yet remained to be enacted, and these were already being drafted to his specifications. The moment Congress adjourned, when he would be released from Washington and could return to Louisiana, they would be rushed to enactment.

Meanwhile he readied his parting shot against the White House. The incident on which he based the grotesque charge that President Roosevelt abetted, or at the very least knew of and acquiesced in, an assassination plot was a supposedly *sub rosa* political caucus held at the Hotel De Soto in New Orleans on Sunday, July 21, 1935. The gathering had been convened presumably without letting any outsider (i.e., "nonplotter") know it was to be held. Its ostensible objective was the selection of an anti-Long gubernatorial candidate whom all anti-Long factions would agree to support against any nominee the Senator might hand-pick for endorsement.

However, with what still appears to be a positive genius for fumbling, the anti-Long leadership guarded with such butter-fingered zeal the secret of whether, where, or when they were to meet that even before they assembled, Long aides had ample time to install the microphone of a dictograph in the room where the anti-Long General Staff was to confer. The device functioned very fuzzily. Its recording (which it was hoped to duplicate and replay from sound trucks throughout the ensuing campaign) was only spottily intelligible. But a couple of court reporters had also been equipped with earphones at a listening post, and their stenographic transcript, though incomplete, afforded some excerpts which Senator Long inflated into what he presented as a full-scale murder plot.

His fulmination was delivered before a crowded gallery, as usual. This popularity annoyed many of his senior colleagues, none more so than Vice-President Garner, whom John L. Lewis was soon to stigmatize as "that labor-baiting, poker-playing, whiskey-drinking evil old man." More than once, as the galleries emptied with a rush the moment Long finished, Mr. Garner would call to the departing auditors, saying: "Yes, you can go now! The show's over!"

In this instance, as on many previous occasions, there was no advance hint of the fireworks to come. The fuse was a debate over the Frazier-Lemke bill, and Senator Long contented himself at the outset with charging that the administration was conducting "government by blackmail." In making this statement he was referring to NIRA, which had succeeded NRA, the latter having been declared unconstitutional some three months earlier. This had nothing to do with the Frazier-Lemke bill, but it gave Mr. Long an opportunity to charge that no contracts for PWA work were being financed unless the contractor agreed to abide by all the provisions of the NRA code which the Supreme Court had invalidated.

That led to the statement that "we in Louisiana have never stood for [such] blackmail from anybody," which in turn led to a section of his arraignment the *Congressional Record* headed:

"THE PLAN OF ROBBERY, MURDER, BLACKMAIL, OR THEFT"

He then loosed his farewell salvo.

"I have a record of an anti-Long conference held by the anti-Long Representatives from Louisiana in Congress," he said in part. "The faithful Roosevelt Congressmen had gone down there to put the Long crowd out. . . . Here is what happened among the Congressmen representing Roosevelt the first, the last and the littlest."

Holding aloft what he said was a transcript of the dictograph record, he listed the names of those present, naming a collector of internal revenue, an FERA manager for the state, and giving as the first direct quote of one of the conferees a statement made by one Oscar Whilden, a burly horse-and-mule dealer who had headed an anti-Long direct-action group calling itself the Square Deal Association. Whilden was quoted as saying at the very opening of the meeting that "I am out to murder, kill, bulldoze, steal or anything else to win this election!"

An unidentified voice mentioned that the anti-Long faction would be aided by more "income tax indictments, and there will be some more convictions. They tell me O. K. Allen will be the next to be indicted."

"That," explained Mr. Long for the benefit of his hearers and the press gallery, "is the governor of Louisiana. Send them down these culprits and thieves and thugs who openly advocate murdering people, and who have been participants in the murder of some people and in their undertaking to murder others—send them down these thugs and thieves and culprits and rascals who have been placed upon Government payrolls, drawing from five to six thousand dollars a year, to carry on and wage war in the name of the sacred flag, the Stars and Stripes. That is the kind of government to which the administration has attached itself in the state of Louisiana!"

Four of Louisiana's congressmen were named as having taken part in the caucus which Senator Long dubbed a "murder conference." They were J. Y. Sanders, Jr., Cleveland Dear, Numa Montet, and John Sandlin. But it was another of the conferees whom Senator Long quoted next, reading from

the transcript, as suggesting that "we have Dear to make a trip
around the state and then announce that the people want
him to run for Governor, and no one will know about this
arrangement here . . . as you all know we must all keep all
of this a secret and not even tell our own families of what is
done." Whereupon, according to the record, another voice
proposed that "we should make fellows like Farley and Roosevelt and the suffering corporations . . . cough up enough to
get rid of that fellow."

Commented Senator Long: "Yes, we should make the
Standard Oil Company and the 'suffering corporations' cough
up enough . . . says Mr. Sandlin . . . [but] I am going
to teach my friends in the Senate how to lick this kind of corruption. I am going to show them how to lick it to a shirt-
tail finish. . . . I am going to give you a lesson in January
to show you that the crookedness and rottenness and corruption of this Government, however ably [sic!] financed
and however many big corporations join in it, will not get to
first base."

More of the same sort of dialogue was read from the transcript. Congressman Sandlin assured the meeting that President Roosevelt will "endorse our candidate." Another of the
conferees, one O'Rourke, was described by Long as having
refused to testify when another witness at an inquiry into
one of Huey Long's earlier murder-plot charges "swore that
he had hired O'Rourke to commit murder in Baton Rouge.
I was the man he was to kill so there was not much said
about it except that he refused to testify on the ground that
he would incriminate himself, whereupon Roosevelt employed him. He was qualified and he was appointed."

The statement most frequently quoted in the weeks and
months that followed was that of an unidentified voice
which the transcript reported as saying: "I would draw in a
lottery to go out and kill Long. It would take only one man,

one gun and one bullet." And some time thereafter, according to the transcript, another unidentified voice declared that
"I haven't the slightest doubt but that Roosevelt would pardon any one who killed Long." Thereupon someone asked:
"But how could it be done?" and the reply was: "The best
way would be to just hang around Washington and kill him
right in the Senate."

The conference was adjourned after notifying Congressman Dear that the people would clamor to have him run
for governor of Louisiana. (The significance of this is that
in one of Dear's final campaign speeches he made the statement that gave rise to a widely disseminated and still per-
sistent version of the shooting that followed, by almost
exactly one month, the delivery of Long's attack on the New
Deal.)

Long concluded his address to the Senate with the asser-
tion that he had exposed this presumably hush-hush meeting
"to the United States Senate and, I hope, to the country
. . . and I wish to announce further they have sent additional inspectors and various other bureaucrats down in the
State. . . .

"The State of Louisiana has no fear whatever of any kind
of tactics thus agreed upon and thus imposed. The State of
Louisiana will remain a state. When you hear from the election returns in the coming January . . . Louisiana will not
have a government imposed on it that represents murder,
blackmail, oppression or destitution."

The Senate then resumed the business of the day. But
most of the correspondents in the press gallery had left and
the talk was all of Huey Long's excoriation of the New Deal,
of his promise that "if it is in a Presidential primary, they
will hear from the people of the United States," and of his
declaration that rumors of the New Deal leaders plotting
to have him murdered were now "fully verified."

NOTE: Most of the purely local references, repetitions, adversions to extraneous matters, and the like have been omitted from the foregoing condensation of Senator Long's last speech before the Senate. Those who may wish to read the full text of his address will find it in the *Congressional Record* for August 9, 1935, pages 12780 through 12791. The section headed "The Plan of Robbery, Murder, Blackmail, or Theft" begins on page 12786, second column.

> *"Behold, my desire is that mine adversary had written a book. Surely I would take it upon my shoulder and bind it as a crown to me."*
>
> ——JOB

Congress did not adjourn its 1935 session until seventeen days after Senator Long had delivered his blast about "the plan of robbery, murder, blackmail, or theft" at the Roosevelt administration in general and at its head in particular. This was, as he clearly stated in his reference to presidential primaries, the opening move in launching his 1936 candidacy for president; the next step would be publication and distribution of *My First Days in the White House.*

He devoted himself to revision of this manuscript during the fortnight in which Congress remained in session, and marveled at the difficulties he encountered. Like many another magnetic orator, he was no writer, and in spite of the ghosts who had helped bring it into being, *My First Days in the White House* eloquently testifies to that fact. None the less, had he lived, the book would have won him adherents by the million. In all its naïve oversimplification, it was still a triumph of classical composition beside the helter-skelter phraseology of his senatorial and stump-speaking oratory. But the latter, like his many other public utterances, his early political circulars, and even the jumbled prose of his first book: *Every Man a King,* had been accepted almost as gospel by Longolators who jeered at literate anti-Long editorials as propaganda dictated and paid for by the Money Barons.

Congress did adjourn in due course, and now it is time to follow Long almost hour by hour through the final ten days of his life, assembling an unbiased chronicle in order to dispel myths and reveal truths about his assassination. His first concern was the publication of his book. His only other fixed commitment before having Governor Allen call the legislature into special session for the enactment of a final dossier of dictatorship laws, was delivery of a Labor Day address at Oklahoma City on September 2. He had accepted this invitation gladly, since it would afford him an opportunity to couple evangelistic grandiloquence about wealth-sharing with kind words about blind Senator Thomas Gore, who faced stiff opposition in his campaign for re-election.

Earle Christenberry was left in charge of the Washington office, where he was to pack for transportation all documents and records which might be needed to elect a Long-endorsed governor and other state officials in Louisiana. Meanwhile, Mr. Long with the manuscript of his book and three of his bodyguards went to New York for a few days of relaxation.

It was also part of his long-range design to seek the Democratic Party's nomination for president at the 1936 convention. To be sure, he was under no misconception as to the sort of fate this bid would encounter. For one thing, Roosevelt's personal popularity had reached new heights as his first term drew to a close. His nomination for a second term was all but inevitable. Long had attacked not only the administration as such. He was carrying on corrosive personal feuds with Postmaster General Farley, Interior Secretary Ickes, NRA Administrator Hugh Johnson, Senate Majority Leader Joe Robinson, and a host of other party bigwigs.

Naturally, Louisiana's Kingfish realized fully that these leaders, controlling the party machinery in the convention of 1936, would see to it not merely that F.D.R. received a virtually unanimous nomination for a second term, but that even were Roosevelt eliminated from contention, Huey Long's effort to become the party's standard bearer would be rejected.

Unquestionably, that is exactly what the Kingfish wanted. He already had a virtually crackproof national organization in his swiftly expanding Share-Our-Wealth clubs. The growth of this movement was now so rapid that his staff found difficulty in keeping pace with it. So valuable had its name become that both "Share *Our* Wealth" and "Share *the* Wealth" were copyrighted in Earle Christenberry's name.

Long's purpose was to rally from both the Republican and Democratic camps the many who were still embittered by their struggles to escape the Great Depression. Times had undeniably bettered. The economy would reach a peak figure in 1937. But even the WPA "shovel leaners" were convinced that the government owed them much more than was being doled out on payday, and were entranced by the vision of a future in which Huey Long would soak the rich to provide for each toiler, however lowly his station, an income of $5000 a year and a span of mules.

In the prairie corn and wheat belts, in the Dakotas and in Oklahoma, in all the places where Long had preached wealth-sharing while campaigning for Roosevelt, desperate landowners on the verge of eviction from mortgaged or tax-delinquent acres their forebears had carved out of the wilderness, were still rallying their friends and neighbors to help keep potential bidders from foreclosure auctions. These too would recall Long's clamorous efforts to bring the Frazier-Lemke bill to a vote, and the conservatives' success in holding it back from the floor. One and all, they would read *My First Days in the White House*, and they would learn in its pages how readily a wealth-sharing miracle could come to pass if only Huey Long were president. . . .

None the less, publishers were chary of bringing out the book under their imprint. To Long this was no matter for concern. Over a period of at least three years a war chest for the presidential campaign he planned to wage in 1936 had been growing steadily. It included not merely money—a levy on the salaries of all public employees under his domination in Louisiana, and major campaign contributions from corporations that felt themselves obligated to show tangible appreciation for past favors or sought to insure themselves against future reprisal—it included also a solid stockpile of affidavits about the boondoggles of divers federal agencies. Hard-pressed men, driven to almost any lengths by the crying need of their families for such bare necessities as food and shelter, were being forced to promise they would "praise Roosevelt and cuss Long" before being granted a WPA laborer's pittance.

At the outset of Long's senatorial career this entire trove of cash and documentary dynamite was kept in some strongboxes of the Mayflower Hotel, where the Senator first established his capitol residence. But for various reasons, at least one of which was the hotel's refusal to bar his political opponents from registering there while in Washington, his relations with the Mayflower deteriorated rapidly to the point where he moved to the Broadmoor, at 3601 Connecticut Avenue. The view from one of the windows of his apartment overlooking Rock Creek Park charmed him. At the same time the campaign cash and documents were transferred to the safety-deposit vaults of the Riggs National Bank, where the Senator kept a Washington checking account, or rather, where Earle Christenberry kept it for him.

Hence the question of paying for the publication of *My First Days in the White House* presented no problem. For that matter, neither did the seeming permanence of a few scattered centers of anti-Long resistance in Louisiana. Since the dictatorship laws enacted during the previous twelve-month made it virtually impossible to defeat Long proposals in the legislature, or Long candidates at the polls, the fixity of a few isolated opposition enclaves was desirable because, to quote Mr. Long, "it gives me somebody to cuss out, and I can't make a speech that's worth a damn unless I'm raising hell about what my enemies are doing."

Only one stubborn stronghold of this sort really irked him by its refusal to capitulate. This was the parish of St. Landry, whose seat was Opelousas. Always independent of alien dictation, this fourth-largest county in Louisiana had remained uncompromisingly anti-Long under the leadership of a couple of patriarchal autocrats: Judge Benjamin Pavy, tall, heavy-set, and wide-shouldered, with a roundish countenance against whose rather sallow complexion a white mustache stood out in sharp contrast; and District Attorney Lee Garland, short and plump, his features pink beneath a flowing crest of white hair.

Garland, much the elder, had held office continuously for forty-four years, Judge Pavy for twenty-eight. The latter had been elected to the district bench in 1908, after an exceptionally bitter local contest in which the leader of the anti-Pavy forces, Sheriff Marion Swords, went so far as to charge that one of Ben Pavy's distant relatives-in-law was an individual the purity of whose Caucasian ancestry was open to challenge. Since Judge Pavy was elected not only then, but continuously thereafter for the next twenty-eight years in election after election, it is obvious the report was given no credence at the time. With the passage of years, the incident was forgotten.

The situation in the parish of St. Landry would not have disturbed Huey Long too greatly, had there not been the

possibility that in some future state Supreme Court election
the heavy vote of that parish might upset the high tribunal's
political four-to-three Long-faction majority. On this ground
alone it might be important for the Kingfish to alter the
political climate of the St. Landry judicial district before the
larger demands of an approaching presidential campaign mo-
nopolized his time and energy.

A matter of prestige was likewise involved. It was Long's
purpose to take the stump personally in the St. Landry area,
in order to bring about the defeat of its heavily entrenched
Pavy-Garland faction and score a personal triumph. On the
other hand, if through some mischance his persuasive oratory
and the well-drilled efficiency of his cohorts failed to carry
the day, the result would be hailed not merely in Louisiana,
but throughout the nation, as a personal defeat for the Kingfish. Hence, nothing must be left to chance. Matters must be
so arranged that failure was to all intents and purposes impossible.

This involved no very serious difficulties. Earlier that summer, when he first outlined to his lieutenants plans for liq-
uidating the Pavy-Garland entente as a politically potent
factor, he gave orders to prepare for a special session of the legislature, this one to be called as soon as Congress adjourned.
Once convened, the lawmakers were to gerrymander St.
Landry from the thirteenth into the fifteenth judicial district.
This would leave Evangeline (Dr. Vidrine's home bailiwick),
small but overwhelmingly pro-Long, as the only parish in the
thirteenth district, thus assuring the election of a friendly
judge there.

At the same time, it would annex St. Landry to another
district which already included three large pro-Long parishes.
Admittedly, the enlarged district would be given two judges
instead of one, but under the new arrangement neither could
possibly be elected without Long's endorsement.

Senator Long took it for granted that his wishes—commands, rather—would be complied with at once. But some close friends earnestly urged him to forgo the gerrymander, at least temporarily. Political feeling was running too high as matters stood to risk possible violence, perhaps even a popular uprising, through such high-handed and summary procedures. Reluctantly, he agreed to hold this particular project in abeyance, but only for the moment.

At the close of August, however, with Congress in adjournment, and in view of the need to neutralize the federal government's policy of patronage distribution solely for the benefit of his political foes back home, he decided that the time for action was at hand. Once more he sent word to Baton Rouge that preparations for a special legislative session, the fourth of that calendar year, be started without further delay. It should be convened on the night of Saturday, September 7.

Meanwhile certain bills, embodying the statutory changes he wanted, should be drafted forthwith by Executive Counsel George Wallace, so that he—Huey—could check their wording in advance, and make any amendments he deemed necessary. This must be done with secrecy—not the sort of puerile intrigue with which his opponents had assembled their hotel conference, but under a tight cloak of concealment, so as to catch the opposition unawares. The gerrymander that would retire Judge Pavy to private life was to be the first measure introduced and passed, becoming House Bill Number One and later Act Number One. The date of the state's congressional primaries was also to be moved up from September 1936 to January. These should be held at the same time as the primaries for governor and other elective state officers. And there was another measure, one still in the planning stage, the details of which he would give later; something to take the sting out of Roosevelt's punitive dispensation of federal patronage in Louisiana.

Having disposed of these matters, Long left Washington for New York with three of his most trusted bodyguards—Murphy Roden, Paul Voitier, and Theophile Landry. All he had in mind at the moment was a day or two of relaxation. August 30 was his birthday. He would be forty-two years old. This in itself called for some sort of celebration. Besides, in view of the busy weeks ahead—the Labor Day speech in Oklahoma on September 2, the special session of the legislature, the need to rush *My First Days in the White House* into print, the fall and winter campaign for state offices, the presidential campaign to follow—this might well be, for no one knew how long, his last opportunity for casual diversion.

"We flew to New York from Washington," Captain Landry recalls, "and went straight to the New Yorker Hotel, where they always put the Senator in a suite on the thirty-second floor. We got there on August 29. I remember that because the next day, a Friday, was his birthday, and Ralph Hitz, the owner of the hotel, sent up a big birthday cake. Lila Lee, a New Orleans girl who was vocalist for Nick Lucas' band that was playing the New Yorker's supper room, came up to the suite with the cake to sing Happy-birthday-dear-Huey. After the cake had been cut and we all had a taste of it, he gave the rest to Miss Lee.

"About that time Lou Irwin came up to take us out to dinner. I think the Senator had talked to him on the phone about finding someone to publish his book, and that Lou had said this was out of his line, since he was a theatrical agent, but he would inquire around and see what could be done. Earle Christenberry wasn't with us. He had remained in Washington to gather up all the things the Senator might need in Louisiana, papers and so on, and he was going to take his time driving home with them while we went on to Oklahoma City.

"Anyway, Lou Irwin said he had just booked a show into some place uptown. I have forgotten the name of it; all I remember is it was quite a ways uptown, and Lou told us they had just imported from France some chef that made the best onion soup in the world.

"So we went there to eat, and we had hardly sat down when who should come over to our table but Phil Baker, the radio star. He said: 'Senator, I want you to meet the two most beautiful girls in New York, my wife Peggy and her niece.' I don't remember the niece's name, but she was a young girl that looked to be about eighteen, and she was very pretty. Baker was all excited, talking about having just signed a contract that very day with the Gulf Refining people to take over their radio show, the one Will Rogers, who got killed in a plane crash with Wiley Post up in Alaska a couple of weeks before that, used to do."

The name of the niece was Cleanthe Carr. Her father, Gene Carr, was one of the best-known cartoonists and comic-strip originators in the country. His work was widely syndicated.

"The Senator got up to dance with Mrs. Baker," the Landry account continues, "and she must have told him, while they were dancing, about this niece being an artist, because when they came back to the table he picked up a napkin and gave it to this girl, saying: 'Young lady, I understand you're quite a cartoonist. Let's see you sketch me here on this napkin!' Well, she made a perfect sketch of him, with his arms out and his hair flying, as though he were making a hell-fire speech. He thought the sketch was fine, but Phil Baker said we ought to see some of her serious work, and we all should come up to his apartment, where he had quite a few of the paintings she had done.

"So we left. I don't think Lou Irwin came with us. But

anyway, after we had been quite a long while at the Baker
apartment, Senator Long said the niece would have to do the
pictures for his book that he had written about how he was
already elected president and what he did in the White House
to redistribute the wealth after he was inaugurated. By the
time we got back to the hotel it was three o'clock in the morning.

"The Senator went over to the newsstand to look at the
headlines in the morning papers, and a gentleman who had
been in the lobby when we came in got up and came over
to me and asked if my name was Captain Landry. I told him
yes, that was right, and he said he wanted to talk to Mr. Long.
I said: 'Man, don't you see what time it is? You haven't got
a chance to see him now. You better come back tomorrow.'

"So he said it was very important for him to talk to the
Senator right away, that he had been sent up from Washington by Earle Christenberry, and that was how he knew what
my name was. He also said he represented the Harrisburg
Telegraph Publishing Company in Harrisburg, Pennsylvania,
and they were anxious to publish the Senator's book about
his first days in the White House. Naturally, that made a
difference, because that was one of the things Senator Long
had come to New York for, so I went across the lobby to the
newsstand and told him what the story was.

"At first he said he wasn't about to talk to anybody that
time of night, but when I told him how Earle had sent the
man up special because the Harrisburg *Telegraph* people
wanted to publish the book, and how the man said he had
just missed us when we went out to supper, and had been
waiting in the lobby ever since, the Senator said: 'Well, all
right, then. Tell him to come up to 3200 in about ten minutes,
but make him understand he'll have to talk damn fast when
he gets there.' So I did, and the man—I have forgotten his
name; that's if I ever knew it—didn't have to talk so fast after

all, because the meeting didn't break up till after five o'clock, when we all just about barely had time to get packed and catch the first train for Harrisburg.

"This was Saturday morning, August 31, and we went from the station at Harrisburg right to the office of the newspaper and I know they must have reached an agreement about printing the book, because when we left by train for St. Louis that evening, two stenographers and a sort of editor from the Harrisburg *Telegraph* came along, and they were working most of the night and all the next morning, cutting down the manuscript for this book. It was too long the way it was written. Anyhow, as I remember, they cut out two hundred pages, and finished just about the time we got ready to cross the bridge and pull into St. Louis, where we only had about five minutes to change to the train for Oklahoma City.

"This was a Sunday morning, and while I don't know how the word had got around St. Louis that Huey Long was passing through, I tell you that old station there was packed and jammed like nobody ever saw before, with people that were not working, it being Sunday, so they just wanted to catch one glimpse of the man while he was passing through."

Senator Long, Theophile Landry, and Paul Voitier, another bodyguard, reached Oklahoma City late that afternoon. Only one public official, Mayor Frank Martin, was at the station to greet the distinguished visitor.

"Officials in Fadeout as Huey Lands" headlined the Oklahoma City *Times*. Most conspicuous among the absentees was State Labor Commissioner W. A. Murphy who, when invited by the local Trades and Labor Council some days earlier to appear jointly with Long as one of the Labor Day speakers, replied:

"I won't be near or in a parade or program with that fellow . . . A man trying to destroy the only President who ever tried to help union labor doesn't deserve the support of labor, let alone being its guest."

Long was suffering from an attack of hay fever and from near-exhaustion when he reached the Black Hotel. He had had almost no sleep since the previous Friday morning. But he was in better spirits the next day when he greeted among others Kaye Dawson, the produce merchant for whom he had been a part-time salesman in Norman during his brief interlude of trying to work his way through the law school of the University of Oklahoma. It is worth noting, however, that when Dawson invited him to visit his home, Long stipulated that both Landry and Voitier be included in the invitation.

He rode in the Labor Day parade that morning, too, and returned to his hotel suite to hold an impromptu press conference about his Share-Our-Wealth program. But when one of the reporters asked him whether he had ever pressed the charge, made only two or three weeks earlier, that several Louisiana congressmen were plotting his death, he snapped:

"I'm tired of talking. If you can't stay here without asking questions, get the hell out. Can't you see I'm tired?"

That afternoon the Labor Day crowd at the Fair Grounds cheered his speech lustily, even his attacks on Roosevelt and Hoover, whom he compared to the peddler of two patent medicines, High Popalorum and Low Popahiram, both being made from the bark of the same tree.

"But for one the peddler peeled the bark off from the top down," he explained, "and for the other he peeled it off from the bottom up. And that's the way it is at Washington. Roosevelt and his crowd are skinning us from the ear down, and Hoover and the Republicans are doing the job from the ankle up. But they've both been skinning us and there ain't either side left now."

"Huey May Toss Hat," headlined the *Oklahoman* next day, and quoted Huey's promise that "if Mr. Roosevelt and Mr.

Hoover are the nominees next year, or anyone that looks like Roosevelt or Hoover, we will have us another candidate."

He left almost immediately after the rally, even though the only available eastbound train would carry him no farther along the road to Louisiana than Dallas. From that point he and his two bodyguards motored to Shreveport, where they were met by another of the bodyguards, George McQuiston, who had been dispatched from Baton Rouge in a state-police car to await the Senator's coming.

They passed the night at the Washington-Youree Hotel, where the Kingfish conferred with his local political satraps. The following morning he and his entourage left for Baton Rouge, arriving in time to begin a day-and-night series of meetings with Governor Allen, George Wallace, Secretary of State Eugene Conway, and others. There Landry and the Senator parted company.

"He said for me to go to New Orleans and rest there, and go on a vacation if I wanted to," Landry added. "He said something about all of us going on a vacation soon, just as soon as things in Baton Rouge got settled. If only I had stayed with him I might have been where I could save his life! But the one thing that never came into my mind was that anybody would try anything in Baton Rouge. Not in Baton Rouge, where he was always surrounded by some of us . . . not in Baton Rouge where you'd think he'd surely be safe. . . ."

> *"There is nothing more diffi-*
> *cult to undertake, more un-*
> *certain to succeed, and more*
> *dangerous to manage, than to*
> *prescribe new laws."*
>
> ———MACHIAVELLI

Tuesday far into the night, throughout Wednesday, and again Thursday until well past noon, Long labored with attorneys, officials, secretaries, and typists, going over and over the measures to be introduced when the forthcoming special legislative session was convened. The streamlined rush with which such bills were speeded to final enactment in less than five days did not allow for delays to correct them once they had been dropped into the hopper.

The system that made this possible was not original with the Kingfish. It had been devised by two astute parliamentarians, Oramel Simpson and George Wallace, to meet the exigencies of a flood crisis in 1927.

By convening the legislature late at night, with all bills whipped into final shape before the lawmakers assembled, having one member introduce all the bills, suspending the rules to have them all referred at once, and all to the same committee, regardless of content, what would otherwise be delayed by being parceled out on two separate legislative days could be accomplished in a matter of minutes.

Then, immediately after midnight, or even the next morning, the committee could meet, gallop through the dossier, give all administration-sponsored measures a favorable report, and turn thumbs down on all anti-administration proposals (the record was forty-four bills thus "considered" in an hour and seven minutes), report them back to the House, and order them engrossed and put on the calendar for final action the next morning. That would be another legislative day.

On the morrow the House would then pass the bills as fast as the clerk could mumble a few words of the title and the members could press the electric-voting-machine buttons. Immediately thereafter the bills would be rushed across the corridor to the Senate, where the same routine would be followed.

Thus the third legislative day in the House would also be the first legislative day in the Senate, so that a few minutes after the fourth midnight, the governor could sign the bills into law, each measure having been read "in full" on three separate days in each house.

This was a brilliant device for meeting an emergency; the iniquity of it lay in the fact that, when employed as routine, it shut off all real study of the proposals, and barred opponents or representatives of the public from being heard on them before committees.

By Thursday noon, September 5, everything was in readiness for the introduction at a moment's notice of thirty-one administration- (i.e., "Long") sponsored must bills—all this without one official word to indicate that a special session was so much as contemplated. None the less, among the press correspondents in the capitol gallery it was taken for granted that such an assembly would be convened at the weekend; but when they pressed Senator Long to confirm or deny the surmise, he professed complete ignorance.

"As far's I know," he said blandly, "Oscar hasn't made up

his mind about if he'll call one any time soon. Leastaways he never said a word to me about it."

"When are you going to make up his mind so he can tell you?" quipped one of the reporters.

"He'd near about kill you if he heard you say that," chuckled the Kingfish good-naturedly, "and his wife would finish the job."

He spent some time then chatting informally with rural well-wishers, while waiting for Murphy Roden, who had driven the Cadillac with License Plate Number 1 from Washington to New Orleans and was to call for its owner that afternoon in Baton Rouge. The Senator was due to make one of his fiery radio broadcasts over a state-wide hookup that night at eight in the Roosevelt Hotel. After a late lunch at the Heidelberg Hotel coffee shop he read the first installment of a biographical sketch of his career which had just appeared on the newsstands that day in the *Saturday Evening Post.* Then at length, with a group of friends and a cadre of bodyguards to see him off, he left for New Orleans. The by-standers urged him in parting to "pour it on 'em, King-fish . . . give 'em hell, Huey, you're just the boy that can do it!" The party reached the Roosevelt barely five minutes before he was scheduled to begin broadcasting.

He spoke that night for a little more than three hours, interrupting the early portion of his program from time to time to say, as was his custom on such occasions:

"This is Senator Huey P. Long talking, and since the lying newspapers won't tell you these things, I'll get the boys to play a little music for the next five minutes or so, and while they're doing that you go call some friends and neighbors on the telephone and let them know I'm on the air, and if they really want the truth they can turn on their radios and tune in."

One of the major proposals he made public that night was

a project for enabling unusually gifted high-school students to continue their education through college at virtually no cost to themselves or their parents. Education for the under-privileged—e.g., the free-schoolbook law—had been one of the most potent elements in the grand strategy of his drive for popular support when he first entered public life. It high-lighted the last public address of his career as well.

"One thousand boys and girls," he pledged, "will be given a practically free college education at L.S.U. next year. We'll se-lect the ones that make the best grades and send them through college, a thousand of them for a starter. I already asked Dr. Smith [Louisiana State University president] whether he could do it beginning this fall, if we came up with a hundred thousand dollars extra for the University appro-priation, and he said, well, he might be able to do it, any-way he would try. So I asked him could he do it if we gave him an extra *two* hundred thousand dollars, and he said yes indeed he sure could. So I told him we would give him *three* hundred thousand dollars just to make sure he had enough."

Of course he attacked the Roosevelt administration at the national level and for its intrusion via patronage into the local arena of Louisiana politics; and equally of course he "poured it on" Mayor Walmsley, Congressman Sandlin, "the whole old plunderbund that you've done got rid of once and that Roosevelt is trying to saddle back onto you."

At intervals the musicians would play "Every Man a King," and Senator Long, who claimed authorship of the lyrics but could not carry a tune, would recite one chorus to the band's accompaniment; and once he recited a chorus of "Sweetheart of L.S.U.," for which he had also written the lyrics to music composed by Castro Carrazo, the state university's bandmas-ter.

At the end of his three-hour stint he was driven to his

home in posh Audubon Boulevard and spent the night there with his family. But he was up and away early enough the next morning—Friday—to eat breakfast in the Roosevelt Hotel coffee shop, talking with an uninterrupted succession of callers while he was at the table, and again in his twelfth-floor suite, access to which could be gained only if one were passed by a succession of bodyguards. Technically, these were officers of the State Bureau of Investigation and Identification, which had come into being during Long's term as governor.

The bill creating it was introduced by an anti-Long member as a nonpolitical measure, at a time when Louisiana had no state constabulary. The jurisdiction of each sheriff and his deputies was restricted to his county. What the backers of the new measure sought was the creation of a force which, working in conjunction with the F.B.I., would have state-wide jurisdiction.

Instead of opposing this, on the ground that it was inspired by political opponents, Long espoused it enthusiastically, and then turned it into a personal elite guard whose powers were broader than those of any mere local peace officer. Certain particularly trustworthy members of the group were assigned to duty as his bodyguards.

They screened all who sought to approach him in his twelfth-floor retreat at the Roosevelt where he remained throughout Friday, busily instructing influential leaders on how best to speed the work of the special session which would be convened on the following night. Earlier he had summoned Earle Christenberry from his home to the hotel, hoping to straighten out his income-tax situation. Two ninety-day postponements on making a return had already been extended to him by the Bureau. However, there would be no further extensions, he was told. A return would have to be made by September 15. None the less, an unending stream of visitors made it impossible for these two to seclude themselves to prepare the belated return.

Much of the day's discussion concerned itself with the potential candidates for the Long slate in the approaching January election. Most of the minor officials—state auditor, register of the land office, commissioner of agriculture, and the like —would be endorsed for re-election as a matter of course. All had been Long stalwarts for years. But under the constitution a governor was prohibited from succeeding himself, and since Justice Fournet's elevation to the state Supreme Court, the lieutenant-governorship had been filled by an acting president pro tem of the Senate.

A number of top-echelon figures in the Long organization each advanced claims to selection as gubernatorial candidate. Each regarded himself as the logical choice.

Meanwhile, as late as Friday afternoon, the Kingfish continued to insist to reporters who inquired about the rumored special session that "Oscar" had not yet told him when or whether a summons to such a legislative assembly would be issued . . . and even while he was telling the newsmen this, highway motorcycle officers were delivering to every rural doorway in the state a circular which had been rushed into print at Baton Rouge two days earlier.

The text on one side of this fly-sheet followed the standard pattern of a Long attack on all who might oppose the program to be furthered by the special session, those who "want to put [us] back into the hands of thugs, thieves and scoundrels, who loaded the state down with debt and gave the people nothing, who kept the people in the mud and deprived their children of education. . . ."

The other side of the sheet bore an equally vehement excoriation of President Roosevelt and his regime, which was using the weight of federal patronage and federal tax money to defeat "our" movement . . . "the man who promised to redistribute the wealth, but we know now he is not going to keep his word. . . ."

He remained in his suite until dinnertime, when he joined Seymour Weiss in the Fountain Lounge, and made an engagement to play golf with him at the Audubon Park Club's course in the morning. To Earle Christenberry's admonition about the inescapable need to file his income tax before the fifteenth he said:

"Come up to Baton Rouge Sunday morning, and we'll work in the apartment in the State House where we won't be interrupted. Bring the papers with you."

He slept well that night—Friday—and rose refreshed to drive out to Audubon Park with Seymour Weiss in the latter's spandy-new Cadillac, which had been delivered only the afternoon before, and would be ruined the next night by the reckless speed with which, not yet broken in, it was driven to Baton Rouge after news of the shooting reached New Orleans.

The morning was pleasant, and Senator Long enjoyed the game to the fullest. An indifferent golfer at best, he played primarily for the thrill of sending an occasional long drive screaming down the fairway. Whenever he achieved this, and more particularly if in doing so he outdistanced his friend Seymour's drive, he shouted with a delight which not even an ensuing flubbed approach could quench.

The game also gave him an opportunity to discuss current developments and problems with one of the few friends he trusted completely. That Saturday he and Weiss seated themselves on a tee bench, and let foursome after foursome go through while they talked in the only relative privacy available to them. What about the federal patronage impasse?

"I told him," Mr. Weiss recalls, "that some of the leaders were worrying. After all, if the Walmsley-Sandlin people were the only ones who could give out those federal jobs . . . And he interrupted me at that point and asked me had I ever heard of the tenth article of the Bill of Rights? Well, of course I had, and told him so. He said yes, everybody had heard of it, but did I realize what was in it?

"Then he went on to explain that while it was only about three lines long, it provided that anything not specifically permitted to the federal government or forbidden to the states by the Constitution was straight-out reserved to the individual states or to the people.

"I said something like all right, so what then, and he said, as nearly as I can remember his words:

" 'So then there's a bill going into that special session tonight—Oscar must have done issued the call by this time—providing a thousand-dollar fine and one hell of a heavy jail term for any federal employee who interferes with Louisiana's rights under Article Ten. So anybody that uses federal funds to interfere with our program is going to be arrested and tried under the law we're about to pass. That'll give them something to think about up yonder.'

"I didn't believe any such law as that could be made to hold water and said so, and even he admitted that it was open to interpretation, though he still thought it was perfectly sound. But he also said it wouldn't make any difference because long before the question could reach the Supreme Court at Washington and be settled, that federal-patronage deal would be so badly scrambled up it wouldn't affect the outcome of our election in January one bit. He also said he had been telling all our people to take every slick dime of Washington money that was offered to them, and then go to the polls and vote for our candidates, because his program would do more for them than they ever would get out of those lousy WPA jobs.

"The main thing he tried to impress on me that morning was that I could forget all my worries about the presidential campaign. 'Everything's in wonderful shape,' he said to me.

'It's never been in better shape. All the money we're going to need we already have in hand, I mean we've got it right now, not just pledges but cash; and on top of that we've got a load of affidavits and other documents about some of the things that have been going on, a stack of papers heavy enough to break down a bullock.'

"As I remember, I asked if this was the material in the vaults of the Riggs National Bank, and that was when he really surprised me. He said no, everything had been taken out of the Riggs vaults just a few days before he left Washington, and put in another place for safekeeping. But he didn't say where he had put it, and I didn't ask. After all, he was the one to decide where he wanted it, and why, and if the time ever came when it was important for me to know where it was, he would tell me. And besides, he was so confident about everything being in the best possible shape, so sure things couldn't be better, that I felt no anxiety about it.

"'We're going to handle the campaign exactly the same way as we did in the West for that double-crossing Roosevelt in 1932,' he told me. 'Between us, we'll pick out the main towns in each state, and you'll go there five or six days in advance and try to line up someone who will serve as chairman of the meeting when I get there.' That is how we did it in 1932, and it wasn't always easy, because hunting for Democrats in the Dakotas in those days, or in Minnesota, was exactly like the old one about the needle in a haystack. In some of those towns there just wasn't a Democrat. But I would stick to it and find someone, no matter who. If the only Democrat I could produce was a truck driver, all right. Huey would have a truck driver for chairman of the meeting he would address on behalf of Franklin Roosevelt for president.

"'It'll be a lot easier this time,' Huey went on while we were talking during that Saturday golf game, 'because you know and I know I make my best speeches when I'm taking

the hide off of somebody. I never could make a decent Fourth
of July oration in my whole damn life. But give me something to raise hell about and somebody to blame for doing it,
like I had when I was campaigning for Mrs. Caraway in Arkansas, and nobody can stop me!

" 'Not only that, but you'll get on the radio and give out
interviews to the newspapers before I hit town, with all that
same old business about this interesting and controversial
personality that's about to come to town, the man they had
been reading and hearing so much about, and they would
have this chance to come out and find out the truth for themselves. Also what date he'll be there and so on, and how he
would talk about a topic of importance to the whole country, and most of all to them, with Joe Whoozis to preside
over the meeting, and that'll draw a big crowd every time, no
matter if they're Democrats or what. And no matter if they're
Democrats or what I'll have every last, living one of them
talking and thinking and voting my way before I get through.'

"You see, all Huey ever wanted was to get a crowd in front
of him. You could leave the rest to him. He had done just
that in Arkansas three years before, and everything was better
organized by 1935. Not only would I be there with arrangements and interviews, but the boys would have come to town
and distributed literature and cartoon circulars to every house
in the place and printed copies of some of Huey's speeches
about share-the-wealth and so on.

" 'We'll do it just like Arkansas, only on a hell of a lot big-
ger scale,' he said. 'We'll have all the copies we need of *My
First Days in the White House* along with the Share-Our-
Wealth book, which we didn't have in '32, and when I come
to town with the sound trucks and deliver the speech of my
life, you just watch them flock over to our side. . . . Yes, sure,
there's enough money to pay for all those books and pam-
phlets and everything else we'll need.'

"How much money was in that box? I haven't any idea, and I don't think anyone else ever knew. It came from all sorts of sources. State and city employees contributed two per cent of their pay for campaign purposes. Those were the so-called deducts. Then there were campaign contributions from people who disliked Roosevelt and believed Huey could whip him, and didn't care whether he called himself Republican or Democrat or Vegetarian, just so long as he licked Roosevelt or made it possible for somebody else to lick him. Also, there were contributions from people who were under obligations to Huey, like the banks he kept solvent in Louisiana. I don't believe even he had any idea how much the total came to. A million, maybe; maybe several millions. All I know for certain sure is that he said for me not to worry about financing the campaign, that we had every round dollar we ever would need of campaign expenses already put away for safekeeping after he took it out of the Riggs bank vaults—and to this day nobody has ever been able to find out what became of it!

"During the course of our game that morning, walking down the fairways, we talked a lot about the governorship too. As I remember it, Huey mentioned a number of names, and some he said just didn't have what it'd take to run a state, and about some he said he didn't want to buck the north Louisiana prejudice against voting for a Catholic for governor, because there was no use making a campaign any harder than you absolutely had to, even if you could win it anyway.

"The one thing he said we'd have to be careful about was that if he picked one of the half dozen or so that regarded themselves each one as the rightful Long candidate, he would make some of the others so sore there would be a chance of a split in the party, and that was one thing he wanted to avoid.

"Well, with all our time out for talking, it was about two o'clock in the afternoon when we finished our round. He had certainly seemed to enjoy it, both the exercise and the chance to talk without having every Tom, Dick, and Harry coming over to interrupt and say he just wanted to shake hands. Also it must have been a relief to be able to talk without worrying about people listening in or repeating what he was supposed to have said.

"We went back to the hotel for lunch. He said there was no need of me coming up to Baton Rouge either that night or the next day, as the first time the bills would come up for passage would be in the House on Monday morning; it would be just routine up to that time. So I said Bob Maestri [State Conservation Commissioner and later for ten years mayor of New Orleans] and I would be in Baton Rouge on Monday morning, and then we parted. Murphy Roden had been waiting to drive Huey to the capitol, and they left, right after lunch. Everything indicated the going would be so smooth and easy. Who could have dreamed that the next time I saw him, only a day later, he would be waiting for Dr. Maes to come up from New Orleans and try to save his life?"

Baton Rouge's hotel lobbies and the State House corridors alike were crowded by the time Murphy Roden and the Senator reached the skyscraper capitol, where they went at once to his apartment on the twenty-fourth floor. He had the state maintain a suite for him there because he felt that at that height the freedom from pollen and dust enabled him to sleep better.

Most of the House members were already on hand, but many of the senators did not trouble to put in an appearance until the following day. Since all bills were to be introduced in the House, the Senate had nothing more momentous on its agenda than to meet, answer roll call, listen to the chaplain's invocation, and appoint two committees. One of these would solemnly inform the governor, and the other the House, that the Senate of Louisiana was lawfully convened and ready for business. Having conveyed this somewhat less than startling intelligence, the token quorum by which a constitutional mandate had been fulfilled could, and in fact did, adjourn until Monday afternoon, at which time all bills duly passed by the lower house would be laid before them.

These would be headed by House Bill Number One, the anti-Pavy gerrymander, and a somewhat similar measure which was designed to keep Congressman J. Y. Sanders, Jr., from returning to his home in Baton Rouge to run for a judgeship. His father, a former governor and congressman, stood at the very head of Huey Long's *bête noire* list. Another measure high on Long's "must" roster made provision for the fact that his current senatorial term would expire unless renewed in the fall of 1936 by re-election.

But in one-party Louisiana, the Democratic primary was the only actual election, even though technically it selected merely a party nominee. Its date was fixed for September by the state election law as this statute currently stood. Obviously, a campaign for a senatorial primary to be held in the fall of 1936 would play hob with Long's plans to run against Roosevelt for the presidency that same season. Consequently, one of Huey's thirty-one must bills amended the state election law by setting the primary's date ahead from September to January. Thus Mr. Long could win the Democratic nomination (equivalent to election in Louisiana) for senator at the year's outset; with that as paid-up political insurance he would be free to devote the balance of 1936 to his presidential campaign.

Another of the must bills is significant in this connection in spite of the fact that it was rooted in a strictly personal grudge, because it so strikingly exemplifies the savagery with

which at an earlier stage of his career Long made Negro affiliation the prime target of political attack.

Dudley J. LeBlanc, a Southwest Louisiana Acadian, had
run for governor several times, had been a legislator off and
on, and would one day become a millionaire as author and
high priest of a nostrum called Hadacol. He and Long had
been allies as members of the Public Service Commission in
the old days, but had fallen out and had been at swords' points
ever since.

Defeated by the Kingfish when he sought to retain his office, LeBlanc organized a burial-insurance society of a type
immensely popular among the Negroes. Since he catered
primarily to this segment of the population, he put in a Negro
nominal president of the "coffin club," as Long invariably
called it. In the columns of his weekly newspaper, *The American Progress*, Long thereafter lost no opportunity to repro-
duce what purported to be one of the brochures issued by
LeBlanc's company, showing pictures of LeBlanc and the
Negro officers of the company together. Ultimately, Long had
a law passed banning from Louisiana that type of insurance
society.

LeBlanc thereafter moved the company's home office across
the state line into Texas, and continued in business. Although
no longer pillorying opponents by reason of Negro affiliation,
Long included in his must bills a prohibition against publishing, printing, or broadcasting in Louisiana any advertising
matter by insurance companies not authorized to do business
in the state.

Occupied with these and a thousand and one other such
minutiae of legislative procedure, Long remained on the main
floor of the capitol that Saturday night until the House adjourned, trailing a nimbus of bodyguards as he dashed back
and forth between Governor Allen's office and the House
chamber. Some of his leading supporters tried vainly to keep

up with him: Dr. Vidrine, "Cousin Jessie" Nugent, Dr. Clarence Lorio, Louisiana State University president James Monroe Smith. These had little to occupy them, for all the must bills were introduced by their "official" author, Chairman Burke of the Ways and Means Committee; and under a suspension of the rules, each was immediately referred to Mr. Burke's committee as quickly as he could say "Ways and Means" and Speaker Ellender could utter a contrapuntal "Any objections? Hearing none, so ordered!"

Thrill seekers behind the railings and in the gallery had anticipated at least some show of oratorical fireworks. Disappointed when they found the proceedings about as exciting as listening to a couple of clerks take inventory in the kitchenware stockroom of a department store, they drifted away and left the capitol for their homes, while Long and the faithful Murphy Roden retired to the Senator's twenty-fourth-floor retreat.

> *"Unto us a child is born, unto*
> *us a son is given, and the gov-*
> *ernment shall be on his shoul-*
> *der and his name shall be*
> *called Wonderful."*
>
> ——ISAIAH

Young Dr. Carl Weiss, his wife, and his baby son occupied a modest home on Lakeland Drive, not far from the capitol, and therefore likewise conveniently near Our Lady of the Lake Sanitarium, where he did most of his surgical work. The capitol had been built on what was formerly the state university campus. From its north façade the windows of the governor's office looked out across a small, artificial body of water, still known as University Lake, to the big hospital on the opposite bank.

Thus Dr. Weiss, Jr., and Huey Long were within but a few blocks of one another when they rose early Sunday morning. Yvonne Pavy Weiss rose early too. Together she and her husband woke, fed and dressed their three-months-old son, Carl Austin Weiss III, and went with him to the home of Dr. Weiss, Sr., where two doting grandparents fondly took over the baby's care, while the young couple went to Mass. As the elder Dr. Weiss put it in a subsequent statement:

"I was with [my son] practically all day. He and his wife came with their baby to our house early in the morning. They left the baby with me and my wife while they went to

St. Joseph's Church for Mass. After that, his wife returned to our house, while my son went to Scheinuk's [a Baton Rouge florist] to inquire about a patient who had consulted him the day before.

"Mr. Scheinuk gave my son a bouquet of flowers, saying he had not sent any flowers when the baby was born, and my son came home saying: 'Look what Mr. Scheinuk sent the baby.' My son and his wife then went to their home, and returned to take dinner at my house at 1 P.M."

Dr. Weiss, Jr., was twenty-nine years old. He had been graduated at fifteen from Baton Rouge High School and had begun his premedical work at Louisiana State University, transferring to Tulane, where he received his academic degree as Bachelor of Science in 1925, and his degree as Doctor of Medicine in 1927.

"He served as an intern at Tulane," his father once related, "and then at the American Hospital in Paris. He studied under the masters at Vienna, and after completing his work in Paris, served at Bellevue Hospital in New York. The last six months of his stay at Bellevue he was chief of clinic. He then came to Baton Rouge to practice here."

He had sailed from Hoboken on the George Washington on September 19, 1928, and returned to New York on May 19, 1930, aboard the *American Farmer*. On his customs declaration, filed when re-entering the United States, he listed $247 worth of purchases made during his twenty months abroad, including twenty dollars' worth of surgical instruments, a forty-five dollar camera, five dollars' worth of fencing equipment, old swords for which he had paid six dollars, and a pistol for which he had paid eight dollars, a small Belgian automatic, made on the Browning patents.

In college and in his postgraduate work he devoted himself to his studies with a single-mindedness that excluded athletics, though he seems to have taken up fencing while abroad, a sport of many European surgeons. One may therefore take it for granted that while at Tulane he neither shared pilgrimages to the wide-open gaming establishments just across the parish line from New Orleans in adjoining areas, nor patronized the peep-hole Joe-sent-me establishments where needled beer, home-brew, raisin wine, and cut whisky were retailed in the sanctified era of national prohibition.

At one time a story was current that he had met Yvonne Pavy while both were students in Paris. This was not the case. She did not leave for France until a year after he had returned to the United States. An honor graduate of Tulane University's Newcomb College for Women, she had been immensely popular in the social and sorority life of her student years. In 1931 she was selected as one of a group of girls who were sent to Paris to represent Acadian Louisiana. At the same time she was awarded on a competitive basis a French-government scholarship to the Sorbonne, and extended her Parisian sojourn to pursue language studies there.

Returning to Opelousas, she was appointed to a teaching position in the grade school at St. Martinville, where Emmeline Labiche, who according to Louisiana tradition was the prototype of Longfellow's Evangeline, had died nearly two centuries before. The following year she went to Baton Rouge to study for her master's degree at the state university, where she taught a French class at the same time.

Short-lived as it then was, her professional teaching career did follow a Pavy family tradition. Her sister Marie taught in one of the Opelousas grade schools, and one of her father's brothers, Paul Pavy, was principal of the high school there until Huey Long, as inflexible in his attitude toward the Pavy family as Judge Pavy was in his attitude toward him, dismissed them out of hand by invoking one of the "dictatorship statutes"—the one requiring the certification of every public-school employee by a Long-controlled state board.

When Carl Weiss, Jr., returned to Baton Rouge, he joined his father in the practice of medicine. However, he was so determined not to capitalize on the wide esteem and affection in which the elder Dr. Carl Weiss was held that for a time he called himself "Dr. C. Austin Weiss." It was not long, however, before he built up a substantial practice on his own account.

During the course of her postgraduate year at Louisiana State University, Yvonne Pavy had occasion to visit the office of the senior Dr. Weiss for treatment of some minor ailment. When the physician learned of her year at the Sorbonne he told her of his son's studies at the American Hospital in Paris. So they met, Dr. Carl Austin Weiss, Jr., and the daughter of Judge Ben Pavy of Opelousas. They fell deeply in love and were married in December 1933. In midsummer of 1935 their son, the third Carl Austin Weiss, was born, and the sense of fulfillment this kindled in the happy young parents was no greater than the affection lavished on him by his grandparents.

That same Sunday morning Huey Long ordered breakfast sent up from the capitol cafeteria to his twenty-fourth-floor suite. He telephoned Earle Christenberry in New Orleans, reminding him of their engagement concerning the income-tax return that must be filed before another seven days passed. Earle had already packed all the necessary papers, the receipted bills, the canceled checks drawn by the Senator against his two accounts, one in the Riggs National Bank at Washington and one in the National Bank of Commerce at New Orleans. Earle customarily made out all the checks for Huey to sign, and deposited the Kingfish's senatorial salary to Long's account.

"Huey and I had signature cards on file at the Riggs bank in Washington and the National Bank of Commerce in New

Orleans," Christenberry explained. "The only checks he wrote were the ones he issued in New York, and the first I would know of it was when the cancelled check came with the monthly statement, or a call from the bank that the account was overdrawn."

Many persons were under the impression that Long also had a large financial interest in a Win-or-Lose Oil Company but, says Christenberry, "to my knowledge as secretary-treasurer of the company, he had no interest in this corporation, and I so testified in federal court. Months after Huey's death one of the stockholders testified that one certificate issued in his name in reality represented Huey's holdings, but if he received dividends they were paid to him in cash by the holder of that stock certificate, by whom the canceled checks were endorsed and cashed."

Earle reached Baton Rouge some time before noon, and prepared to go over all the papers with his friend and employer. But within a short time, the work being little more than well begun, Long threw up his hands in a characteristic gesture, as though brushing a distasteful matter out of existence.

"He said to me," reported Mr. Christenberry, " 'You know what this is all about, don't you?' and I said I did. 'Well, all right then,' he told me, 'you take all this stuff back to New Orleans with you and fill out the forms, and then bring the whole thing back Monday or Tuesday, and I'll sign the damn papers and we'll be rid of them. Look, I'm not even going to stay here till the end of this session. I'll leave Tuesday, maybe even tomorrow, right after the House passes the bills, and come down to New Orleans and sign them there. And you know what we'll do then? We'll go on a vacation together, just you and me, no bodyguards or anything. We'll get in your car and go wherever we want to go without making one single, slivery plan in advance.'

"After that, he and I went down to the cafeteria and had lunch. Naturally, there was the same steady procession as always of people coming to the table to say hello, but not so many as there would have been any other time except Sunday noon. Most of the legislators and out-of-town politicians would not be in till later that evening because the Senate was to be in recess till Monday and the House wasn't going to meet till eight, and it was going to be just a short session to order the bills put on the calendar for the next morning."

John Fournet was one of the out-of-town notables whose arrival that evening was expected. He had been a member of the Long peerage for years, but had refrained from political activity of that sort ever since his elevation to the state Supreme Court a year or so earlier.

None the less, he had been Speaker of the House for four years, he had been elected to the lieutenant-governorship on the Long-supported Allen ticket in 1932, and was one of those whose name was frequently mentioned as Long's likely choice for endorsement to become Oscar Allen's successor.

Senator Long had requested him to come to the capitol for a conference, and he had left New Orleans early that morning for the home of his parents in Jackson, planning to invite his father to accompany him to Baton Rouge. It would be a proud thing for the elder Fournet to see the deference paid his son as a state Supreme Court justice, as an intimate of the Kingfish, and perhaps as a candidate for governor of Louisiana.

"This day may be the last to any of us at a moment."

———HORATIO NELSON

The thirty-one must bills which were certain to be enacted into law within no more than three more days were the subject of Sunday's mealtime talk throughout Louisiana that noon. Huey Long was expressing complete confidence as to what these would do to "put a crimp into Roosevelt's notion he can run Louisiana." Everyone who paused at his table in the capitol cafeteria was given the same heartening assurance.

In private homes everywhere authentic information as to what the new laws would provide was available for the first time on this day. In New Orleans, Baton Rouge, Monroe, Alexandria, Shreveport, and Lake Charles the morning papers had carried full accounts of the introduction of these measures, giving the subject matter of each bill in summary form.

Thus the members of the Weiss family at last had before them full information about the measure which would displace the father of young Mrs. Weiss from the judicial position he had held continuously since before she was born. But the table talk at the senior Dr. Weiss's home was anything but dispirited.

"My son ate heartily and joked at the dinner," he said when referring to the occasion; and this was borne out in a statement by Yvonne's uncle, Dr. F. Octave Pavy, who was in

Baton Rouge for the session as one of St. Landry parish's
three House members.

In any case, while the gerrymander was not ignored in the
Weiss family conversation, it was not looked upon as a dis-
aster; and after dinner all five—three men named Carl Austin
Weiss and the wives of the two older ones—motored to the
Amite River where Dr. Weiss, Sr., had a summer camp.

Frequently on such occasions, but by no means always,
Carl and Yvonne took with them the small-caliber Belgian
automatic pistol he had brought back from abroad and customarily kept in his car when he went out on night calls.
He and his wife would engage in target practice, shooting at
cans either while these were stationary or as they floated down
the placid current of the river.

But on this particular Sunday they did not bring the gun.
Carl and Yvonne went swimming and had a gay time of it,
while the elders, seated on the warm sand of the high bank,
dandled their wonderful three-month-old grandson.

"While they were swimming," Dr. Weiss, Sr., recalled later,
"I remarked to my wife: 'That boy is just skin and bones,'
and she said: 'Yes, we have got to make him take a rest, he
has been working too hard lately.'"

Seeing them there, that pleasant afternoon, any observer
would have concluded that this was a family group whose
members gave no indication of being troubled by forebodings
of an impending disaster.

Obviously the wonderful baby must have had a feeding
and an occasional change sometime during the afternoon,
and no doubt he slept in his mother's arms once the party
tidied up the camp ground, got into the car, and headed
homeward a little after sundown.

In his high apartment Huey Long, who had not left the
capitol since Murphy Roden drove him to Baton Rouge

from New Orleans on the previous afternoon, gathered his top legislative and political leaders for a consultation about the candidate his faction should endorse for governor. His brother Earl was not among those present, nor was he under consideration for any elective office. The breach between them stemmed from the time Earl ran for lieutenant governor on an anti-Huey ticket three years before.

Justice Fournet, who stood high in the Kingfish's favor, was not present at the conference either. He did not reach the capitol until well after dark. Another absentee was Judge Richard W. Leche of the Circuit Court of Appeal, but——

"Huey had telephoned me to come up for the session," he said in recalling what he could of the day's events. "However, I had been thrown from a horse just a fortnight or so before, while vacationing with Mrs. Leche in Arizona. The fall fractured my left upper arm just below the shoulder. Huey had joked with me about it, saying it was a pity I hadn't broken my neck instead, and I replied that this illustrated once more his readiness to make any sacrifice for the good of the state.

"When he asked me if I would come to Baton Rouge for the session, I assumed this was because I had been Governor Allen's secretary and knew all the legislators. But since it was hardly proper for a judge of the appellate bench to be a lobbyist even on behalf of the administration to which he owes his position, I told him that with my left arm in an airplane splint it was almost impossible for me to get around, and that I would have to stay in New Orleans right along to have dressings changed, and the like. He didn't seem pleased, but nothing more was said about it at the time.

"However, when he called me at my home in Metairie Sunday afternoon he had something else in mind. The first thing he asked me was: 'Dick, what the hell are you, outside of being an Indian?' For a moment this had me stumped. I

couldn't imagine what he meant. Then I remembered that
two or three years earlier, a group of us were chatting about
one thing and another, and the question of religion came up.
That was one thing Huey never bothered about. I mean what
any man's religious beliefs were. Anyway, someone in the
crowd asked me what my religion was. I answered that as
I saw it, religion was something that dealt with the hereafter, and the only people who had a hereafter I thought I
could enjoy were the Indians. They believed in a happy
hunting ground, and as for me, give me a gun and a dog and
some shells and you could keep your harps and your wings.
Anyway, I said I guessed that by religion I would be classed
as an Indian. So when Huey asked me over the phone what
I was, aside from being an Indian, I said:

"'You mean you're asking me what my religion is?'

"'That's exactly what I mean,' he answered. 'You're going
to be my candidate for governor, and some of the boys here
said I couldn't run you because you're a Catholic and it's too
tough to swing north Louisiana's vote to a Catholic for
governor.'

"'Well, I was born a Catholic,' I told him.

"'You didn't run out on them, did you?' he demanded.

"'No,' I told him, 'but I changed to the Presbyterian
church a long time back. Now listen, Huey. I've got no idea
of running for governor. I've got exactly the kind of position I like, and down here they make a practice of re-electing
judges who have not been guilty of flagrant misconduct, so my
future's secure.'

"He said something about how I had better leave all that
to him, and he would see me in New Orleans as soon as the
session was over and we would talk further about it. That
ended the conversation. I never spoke to him again."

Another of the intimates Huey Long summoned to Baton

Rouge that afternoon was Public Service Commissioner (now Juvenile Court Judge) James P. O'Connor. The reason for this was never disclosed, for when O'Connor arrived "we just chatted about a lot of inconsequentialities. One of the things he was all worked up over was writing some more songs with Castro Carrazo for the L.S.U. football team."

The afternoon wore on. Apparently Judge Leche was the only one in whom the Senator confided about the gubernatorial selection.

"Senator Long did not leave the capitol all day," Murphy Roden says in telling about the events in which he played so large a role. "As long as he was in his apartment there was no break in the stream of people who came to call on him. The House was to meet that night and approve the committee's favorable report on the bills so they could be passed and sent to the Senate the next day.

"After he dressed, the Senator was in and out of the apartment, spending some of the time in Governor Allen's office. I brought his supper up to him from the cafeteria, and several persons were there talking to him while he ate, but no one ate with him. He went down to the governor's office about seven o'clock, even though the House wasn't scheduled to meet until eight."

> *"The results of political changes are hardly ever those which their friends hope or their foes fear.*
>
> ——THOMAS HUXLEY

Huey Long came down to the main floor of the capitol an hour before the House was to go into session to arrange for an early morning caucus of his followers the next day. Primarily he wanted to make certain that there would then be no absentees among votes on which he knew he could rely.

At regular sessions of the legislature, when House and Senate were normally convened during the forenoon, such early conferences were daily affairs. But since in this instance the ordinary routine did not apply, he was bent on making assurance doubly sure.

Behind closed doors he always took charge of caucuses in person, outlining step by step what was to be done on that particular day: who should make which motions, at what point debate should be cut off by moving the previous question, how the presiding officer was to rule on certain points of order, should these be raised by the opposition, and so on.

Since the next morning's session of the House would be the only genuinely important one of the current assembly, the one at which all thirty-one must bills were to be passed and sent on to the Senate, he was taking no chances on unexpected difficulties due to absenteeism. Not only must every one of his partisans be in his seat when the Speaker called the House to order, but all the House whips and other aides must attend the morning's caucus without fail, to rehearse in the most minute detail every procedural step to be taken on the House floor, and every counter to each procedural obstacle any anti-Long member might seek to raise.

That Sunday evening, seated at Governor Allen's desk, Long was sending for his legislative leaders, one by one, and giving them the names of the men they each had to bring to the caucus by eight the next morning.

Meanwhile, as nearly as can be determined, the five members of the Weiss family returned from their Amite River outing shortly after nightfall. The young physician and his wife left his parents' home with the baby for their own Lakeland Avenue residence. A composite of various subsequent accounts pictures the scene there as one of tranquil domesticity.

Yvonne prepared the baby for bed while Carl went out to the yard and remained there for a time, petting the dog. Coming back indoors about 8:15, he made a telephone call to his anesthetist, Dr. J. Webb McGehee. Yvonne assumed that this call was to a patient, but Dr. McGehee later confirmed the fact that Dr. Weiss called "and asked me if I knew that the operation for the following day had been changed from Our Lady of the Lake Sanitarium to the General Hospital. I told him I knew that."

Miss Theoda Carriere, one of the registered nurses later called to attend Senator Long, lived not far from the home of Dr. Weiss. After a twelve-hour day stint at the Sanitarium, in attendance on a traffic-accident victim, she was taking her ease on the front gallery of her home. She saw Dr. Weiss leave his house at this time, and depart in the direction of Baton

Rouge General Hospital. There he checked the condition of the patient on whom he was to operate the next day.

In view of the time factor involved, he must have gone from the hospital directly to the State House, leaving his car in the capitol's parking area, where it was found later. At least five eyewitnesses place him in the north corridor of the capitol's main floor a little before 9:30, waiting in a shallow niche opposite the double door to Governor Allen's anteroom.

Charles E. Frampton is now manager of the State Museum at the Cabildo in New Orleans, the building in whose *sala capitular* the transfer of Louisiana from France to the United States was consummated. But in 1935 he was one of the veterans of the press gallery at Baton Rouge. He describes what he saw as follows:

"Some time after eight o'clock on this particular Sunday night I was seated with Governor Allen at his desk when George Coad, then editor of the *Morning Tribune* in New Orleans, called me by phone from the office and said a hurricane had wrecked a Civilian Conservation Corps camp in southern Florida, and that a number of ex-soldiers had been drowned. He asked me if Senator Long was there, and I said I believed he was in the House chamber. Then he asked me to tell him about the storm, and the CCC disaster, and get any comment he might want to make. I told Coad to hold the line; I thought I could get Huey on the phone.

"I picked up another phone on the governor's desk and called the House sergeant-at-arms. Joe Messina answered and said yes, the Senator was right there. I asked if I might talk to him, and he told me to wait a minute. After an interval Huey got on the phone. I relayed what Coad had told me, and asked if he cared to comment on it. He said, 'Hell, yes! Mr. Roosevelt must be pretty happy tonight, because every ex-soldier he gets killed off is one less vote against him.' We chatted for a minute or so longer, and I asked whether he intended to do anything about this when he got back to Washington, and he replied by asking where I was. When I told him I was in Oscar Allen's office, he said: 'Wait there. I'm coming there myself in just a few minutes.'

"I hung up, picked up the other phone, and relayed the conversation to Coad, telling him that since Huey was on the way over I might have an add for him, and to hang on the line. He said he would, and again I laid down the phone without breaking the connection.

"Oscar and I talked for a couple of minutes, and then I thought to myself I had better not wait for Huey to come to me; after all, he was a United States senator and I was a reporter looking for a story, so maybe I'd better go see him. Telling Coad to hang on, I then went out of the governor's private office into the big reception room adjoining it, and opened one of the double doors leading into the corridor that extends from the House chamber to the Senate. As I opened the door this whole thing blew up right in my face."

Justice Fournet takes up the narrative at this point. Here is his statement:

"In the late afternoon my father and I drove from Jackson to Baton Rouge, and I went to the twenty-fourth floor of the capitol in search of Huey. He was not in his apartment, so I returned to the main floor, and looked into the House chamber, where I was informed the Senator was. Sure enough, he was there on the House floor, followed or attended by Joe Messina and talking to Mason Spencer.

"Just as I caught sight of Huey he rushed to the Speaker's rostrum and began to talk with Ellender. When he left there it looked to me as though the House was about to adjourn. Huey rushed by Joe Messina and me. We tried to follow as best we could and got into the north corridor, into which the

February, 1935: On the Speaker's rostrum in the House chamber at Baton
ouge, Huey Long is shown with Hermann Deutsch. Left, Speaker (now U.S.
enator) Allen J. Ellender; right foreground (back to camera) Executive Counsel
eorge M. Wallace.   (LEON TRICE)

BAGGAGE DECLARATION AND ENTRY

384139

BEFORE FILLING OUT THIS DECLARATION READ CAREFULLY INSTRUCTIONS ON BACK OF THIS SHEET
IF SPOILED OR MUTILATED, RETURN TO PURSER OR VESSEL

N°

Name of Passenger Carl Austin Weiss   *Vessel* American Farmer *Port of Arrival* New York

I, the undersigned, declare that I am a resident of the country of United States of America

that I resided in said country from Dec. 18, 1905 to Sept. 19 1928

that I reside at No. 535 Street Fifth City Baton Rouge State La.

that I am a citizen of the country of United States of America; that I last sailed from the United

States on S. S. Geo. Washington on Sept. 19 19 28 from New York (Hoboken)

that I am accompanied by the following-named members of my family and household who are included in this declaration;

that I and those who accompany me are all residents of the same country and our baggage is enumerated below:

BAGGAGE:	NUMBER OF TRUNKS	HAND PACKAGES, VALISES, BAGS, ETC.	BALES, BOXES, BUNDLES	OTHER PACKAGES	TOTAL PIECES OF BAGGAGE	LETTER UNDER WHICH BAGGAGE WILL BE PLACED ON PIER
	1	2				

TO BE FILLED OUT BY PASSENGER Description of articles	PRICE PAID OR FAIR VALUE IF GIFTS, ETC.	FOR CUSTOMS OFFICER'S NOTATIONS ONLY		
		Value	Rate	Duty
2 O'coats $15 and 30.	$45.00			
shoes	10.00			
nat & gloves $4.	9.00			
books	12.00			
surgical insts.	20.00			
camera and equipment	45.00			
pistol	8.00			
fencing equipment	5.00			
old swords	6.00			
ivory statuette	8.00			
table linens	55.00			
lingerie	15.00			
perfume	4.00			
misc. gifts (briquettes etc)	10.00			

TOTAL OF THIS SHEET   TOTAL OF THIS SHEET

Carried forward from continuation sheet   Carried forward from continuation sheet

TOTAL DECLARED   Cashier's Stamp   TOTAL DUTY OR FINE $

DECLARATION OF RETURNING RESIDENT OF THE U. S.

I further declare that I have fully set forth herein all articles acquired abroad, used or unused, whether purchased or otherwise obtained, contained in my baggage or on my person or in the baggage of or on the persons named above accompanying me, that none of the said articles is for sale, traded as a commission for another, or is to be used in business, except as noted hereon; that the value as set forth represent the prices actually paid for purchased articles, or, in the case of articles otherwise obtained, the fair value thereof to the best of my knowledge and belief; that this declaration is made with the knowledge that failure to declare any article acquired abroad or any false statement in regard thereto will subject me to personal penalties and the articles involved to seizure. I further declare that I have not during the past 30 days received an exemption from duty such as is allowed a returning resident of the United States, except as follows:

(signed) Carl Austin Weiss

, Passenger.

Declared to before me 5-19-30 193   , and baggage examined and found correct unless otherwise noted.
Number of packages examined 3 and number of stamps used 3
A. N. Lamont , Inspector.

Baggage stamps Nos.

DECLARATION OF NONRESIDENT OF THE U. S.

I further declare that I have fully set forth herein all the articles in my baggage or on my person, or in the baggage of or on the persons named above accompanying me, that are NOT wearing apparel, articles of personal adornment, toilet articles, and similar personal effects, and all articles that are intended directly or indirectly for sale or for the use of any other person, together with the prices actually paid for purchased articles, or, in the case of articles otherwise obtained, the fair value thereof to the best of my knowledge and belief; and that this declaration is made with the knowledge that failure to declare any such article or any false statement in regard thereto will subject me to personal penalties and the articles involved to seizure.

, Passenger.

VALUE AND DUTY AS NOTED ABOVE

, Appraiser's Examiner.

, Acting Deputy Collector.

2   Official transcript (not the original) of customs declaration filed by Dr. Weiss on returning to this country from medical studies abroad. The seventh item on it is the Belgian automatic found beside his lifeless hand after Huey Long was shot.

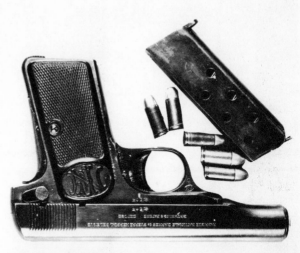

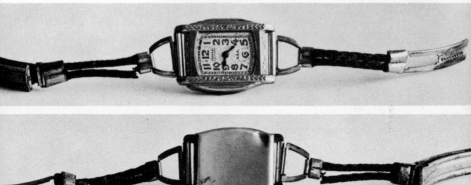

3 Dr. Weiss's pistol, which normally holds seven cartridges, contained only
five unfired ones (and an empty, jammed in the ejector) when it was picked
up after the shooting.

4 & 5 The watch which was shot from Murphy Roden's wrist while he was
grappling with Dr. Weiss. The dial shows the time of the struggle, the dent
in the back was obviously made by a small bullet.

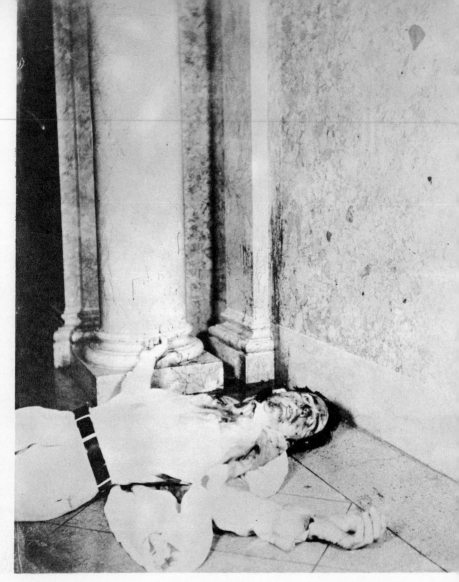

6 No "small blue punctures" were left by the bullets of bodyguards who mowed down Dr. Weiss in the niche where he had waited for Senator Long. The photograph was made after authorities, seeking to establish his identity, had turned over the body which fell face down.

The funeral cortege, moving from the capitol to a newly prepared crypt
which is now the site of a monument. Right foreground, the L.S.U. student
and playing "Every Man a King" in a minor key as the Kingfish's dirge.

8 Huey Long's casket, as it was borne down the capitol's 48 granite steps, followed by members of his family. The two leading pallbearers are (left) Seymour Weiss and Governor Oscar Allen.

9 Laborers work around the clock to prepare a vault in time for Huey Long's funeral, as crowds wait on the capitol steps to file past the bier where his body lies in state.

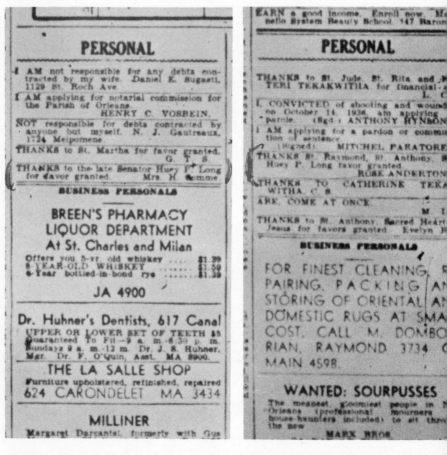

10 & 11   Huey Long was enshrined as a saint by some of his followers as shown by these personals from want-ad pages of the *Times-Picayune*. The one at left appeared on March 26, 1936, the other on January 11, 1937.

House and Senate cloakrooms, the Speaker's and lieutenant governor's office, as well as the governor's office and those of his secretary and executive counsel all open.

"There was not a soul in that corridor when we got there except Louis LeSage and Roy Heidelberg, who were seated on the ledge of the window at the east end of the corridor. I asked them where Huey had gone and they said he was in the governor's office, so Joe and I walked to the door of that office at a leisurely pace, and as we approached the door I could hear a voice which I recognized as that of Senator Long ask:

"'Has everybody been notified about the meeting tomorrow morning?' and a voice which I identified as that of Joe Bates of the Police Bureau of Identification answered: 'Yes, Senator.'

"At this point I noticed three or four people lined up against the marble recess in the corridor wall opposite the door to the governor's anteroom. I don't remember the exact number but I definitely recall there were more than one. Just then Huey walked out of the office door of the governor's secretary and . . ."

The third eyewitness to what took place was Elliott Coleman, on special assignment as one of the Senator's bodyguards and later for many years sheriff of Tensas parish. He says of the night in question:

"I was an officer of what was then known as the Bureau of Criminal Identification, which was headed by General Louis F. Guerre. He had directed me to come from my home in Waterproof for duty at the state capitol during the special session of the legislature. There was nothing specific of an alarming nature, but there was a general feeling of uneasiness in view of the murder-plot probe against the Senator earlier that year, after the Square Deal Association disorders.

"Nothing particularly noteworthy happened on Saturday, but on Sunday night, when the special session was meeting, I went into the House chamber and was standing back of the railing with State Senator Jimmie Noe, and he was trying to get me to help him in his effort to get Huey's endorsement as a candidate for governor in the campaign that was about to begin.

"Huey was in the House, circulating about the floor, talking to this member and to that, with Murphy Roden and George McQuiston remaining outside the railing but as near to him as they could. Huey was talking to Mason Spencer and they were probably joking with each other, or telling a funny story, because they laughed, and then Huey went up on the rostrum and sat with Speaker Allen Ellender for a time. All this while I was outside the railing with Jimmie Noe, and he was talking about getting Huey to back him for governor.

"While Jimmie was talking to me, Huey jumped up all of a sudden, from where he was seated on Ellender's rostrum, and hurried down the side to the corridor. I figured the House was about to adjourn, so I left Jimmie and turned to hurry into the corridor myself. There were not many persons there and I saw Huey, followed by Murphy Roden, go into Allen's office, and it seemed to me like he wasn't in there hardly at all, that it was almost as if he had turned right around and come back out. He was met as he came out by Justice Fournet, and they were walking toward the elevator and toward where I was standing, with Murphy Roden following."

Judge James O'Connor's testimony logically follows that of Sheriff Coleman. He says:

"I was in the House chamber when Huey came sort of storming in and sat down beside Allen Ellender on the rostrum. I was standing in the space between the railing and the wall, chatting with friends, when Huey beckoned to me as though saying: 'Come on over, I want to talk to you.'

"When I got there he said something that struck me as unusual, because he had not been smoking in months, maybe not in as much as a year. He said: 'I want you to get me half a dozen Corona Belvedere cigars.' I asked him where to get those, and he said: 'Downstairs in the cafeteria. They have a box of them there.'

"When I came downstairs something else struck me as very peculiar. There wasn't a soul in that basement on this Sunday night. I walked into the cafeteria. They had just air-conditioned it, and the new glass doors were very heavy. There was no one in that restaurant either, except three or four of the girls behind the counter. I got the cigars and then sat down to drink a cup of coffee, and was about to finish it, when I heard a noise like cannon crackers going off. It was coming faintly through those heavy glass doors. . . ."

Murphy Roden, who recently retired as Superintendent of State Police with the rank of colonel, is last of the surviving eyewitnesses to take up the tale. A graduate of the F.B.I. school and therefore a specially trained observer, his memory is sharp and vivid in recalling what took place during the violent interlude in which he played so large a role. He says:

"Whenever the Senator returned to the governor's office I would wait in the anteroom, and as he went out I would leave just ahead of him, and Elliott Coleman would walk just behind him. He made several trips into the House chamber and back while the House was briefly in session that night.

"On the last such trip the Senator spent a little time on the floor, talking jocularly to several of the members, and then sat for a time with Speaker Ellender on the rostrum. At such times I would follow his movements as best I could from outside the railing, and when he hurried out I would try to anticipate his movements so as to be just ahead of him when he left the hall. The House seemed to be about ready to adjourn then, and he rose and hurried from the rostrum toward the governor's office. I was ahead of him and when he turned in I went into the anteroom and waited for him there. He went into the inner office where Governor Allen was. Joe Bates, a special agent of the Bureau of Criminal Identification and Investigation, and A. P. White, the Governor's secretary, were in there too, along with some other persons whose identity I do not recall except for Chick Frampton of the *Item*, who was standing over Allen's desk and using the telephone in there.

"Senator Long was in that office only a moment or two. It seemed to me as though he had walked right in, turned around, and gone right out, going through the anteroom and heading back toward the hallway. I realized he was going back out, and managed to get into the hall just ahead of him, so as to be in front of him when he got out there. But he was walking fast and caught up to me and was just about beside me at my left. We are speaking now in terms of my being just one step ahead of him as he came out.

"Judge Fournet was standing at the partly opened door that led from the hallway directly into the governor's inner office, a private entry and exit to that office. Behind us was Elliott Coleman. Chick Frampton had also hurried out of the governor's outer office and anteroom right behind us. The Senator was going back in the direction of the House chamber from which he had just come, and from which people were just beginning to move out. But at the private door to Governor Allen's inner office he stopped, and we were standing still as Judge Fournet came up and started to talk to him. I have no idea what they were talking about, because I was not watching them or paying attention, but looking around us as always to see what other persons nearby were doing.

"One of them was a young man in a white linen suit. . . ."

It is 9:30. One floor below, in the otherwise deserted basement cafeteria, Judge O'Connor is still sipping the last of his coffee when, muffled by distance and the heavy glass doors of the restaurant, he hears a noise like exploding cannon crackers.

> "Do we ever hear the most
> recent fact related in exactly
> the same way by the several
> people who were at the same
> time eye-witnesses to it? No."
> ——LORD CHESTERFIELD

The stage is set for a violent climax. Huey Long has turned through the anteroom of the governor's office, where Chick Frampton, bending over the desk with his back to the door, is preparing once more to lay down the telephone without breaking the long-distance connection to New Orleans. He has told his editor, Coad, to hang on while he—Frampton—goes in search of the Senator, and does not see Huey just behind him. Intent on his conversation with Coad, he has heard neither the Senator's question as to whether everyone has been notified about the morning's early caucus, nor Joe Bates's affirmative reply.

By the time he puts down the telephone and turns, Huey Long has already dashed out into the hallway where John Fournet steps forward to greet him. The Senator stops momentarily to talk to A. P. White in the partly opened private doorway to the inner office. He has noticed, while looking over the House from the Speaker's rostrum, that some of his legislative supporters are absent, and asks White where the hell this one, that one, and the other one are, adding: "Find them. If necessary, sober them up, and have them at that

meeting because we just might need their votes tomorrow!"
Then he turns, facing the direction of the House chamber.

For that one fractional moment every actor is motionless:
Huey Long, with John Fournet at his left elbow and Murphy
Roden just behind his right shoulder; Chick Frampton in the
very act of stepping into the corridor from the double doors
of the governor's anteroom; Elliott Coleman down the hall
in the direction of the House, near the door of the small
private elevator reserved for the governor's use; and among
three or four individuals standing in the marble-paneled niche
recessed into the wall opposite the double doors where Frampton is standing, a slim figure in a white suit.

The fractional moment passes. Let us turn once more to
Murphy Roden's graphic account of what transpired:

". . . a young man in a white linen suit, who held a straw
hat in his hand loosely before him, and below the waist, so
that both of his hands seemed to be concealed behind it. He
walked toward us from the direction of the House chamber
and I did not see the gun until his right hand came out from
beneath his hat and he extended the gun chest high and at
arm's length. In that same instant I realized that this was
no jest, no toy gun, and leaped. I seized the hand and the gun
in my right hand and bore down, and as I did so the gun went
off. The cartridge ejected and the recoil of the ejector slide
bruised the web of my right hand between thumb and fore-
finger, though I was not conscious of the hurt and did not see
the injury, a very minor one, until later.

"I tried to wrest the gun away, but saw I could not do it in
time, so shifted my grip on it from my right hand to my left
and threw my right arm around his neck. As I did this, my
hard leather heels slipped on the marble floor and my feet
shot out from under me, so that we both went down, the
young man and I, with him on top. That is the last pair of
hard leather heels I have ever worn. While we were falling,

my wrist watch was shot off, but again I was not conscious of it. I did not even miss my watch until I was being treated at the hospital, later that same night.

"It has always been my belief that it was Dr. Weiss who fired a second shot as we were falling and that it was this one which shot off my watch. There are several reasons for this conclusion on my part. Firstly, his gun was of small caliber, 7.6 millimeter, which is about the equivalent of our .32-caliber automatic, a Belgian Browning which he had brought back with him from abroad. When it was examined later, it had only five cartridges in it. Normally it holds seven. I have always had a deep conviction that Dr. Weiss fired twice, and that I saw the first shell ejected. When his gun was recovered from the floor, a shell was found caught in the ejecting mechanism which I am convinced was the second shell. The dent on my watch, which was later recovered and which I still have, was made by a small-caliber bullet.

"As we were falling—Dr. Weiss and I—I released his gun hand, and reached for my pistol, a Colt .38 special on a .45 frame, loaded with hollow-point ammunition, which I carried in a shoulder holster. By the time we hit the deck I had it out and fired one shot into his throat, under his chin, upward into his head and saw the flesh open up. I struggled to get out from beneath him, and as I partially freed myself, all hell broke loose. The others may have waited till I got partially clear before they fired, for I think I got to my knees by the time they started, and that probably saved my life. But I was being deafened and my eyes were burning with particles of powder from those shots.

"Moreover, for all I knew this might have been an attack in force, which was why I was struggling so desperately to get to my feet. But by the time I really was on my feet, I could not see any more because of the muzzle blasts from other guns. While I did not learn this until later, shots had passed so close to me that the powder burns penetrated my coat, shirt, and undershirt, and burned my skin beneath, all along my back. I felt my way blindly down the hall in the direction of the Senate chamber, with my left hand on the corridor wall and my gun still in my right hand, till I turned a corner and reached a niche where there was a marble settee. This was right near the stairway where Huey had gone down, as I learned later. I was practically blinded for the time. The settee had a padded seat, and I waited there till Ty Campbell, a state highway patrolman, saw me and took me to the hospital.

"It was there that I missed my watch and saw the furrow plowed across the back of my wrist where the scar of it is still visible; also the pinch or scratch in the web between my right thumb and index finger. I did not know for two days what had become of my watch, but it was returned to me later by King Strenzke, chief of the Baton Rouge city police. Someone had picked it up off the floor at the scene of all the shooting, and had turned it over to the police while authorities were still trying to establish the identity of Dr. Weiss."

Justice Fournet's statement differs from Roden's at several points, as it does from the accounts of Coleman and Frampton, each of which differs in one detail or another from all the others. Just as it was given, with none of the discrepancies modified, altered, or omitted, the Fournet account of what took place continues in the narrative which follows:

". . . Just then, Huey came out of the door to the office of the Governor's secretary." (Actually, he had come out of the main double doors of the anteroom, and was merely pausing at the other point to impress on White the importance of getting in touch with certain absentee members.) "We walked toward each other, but instead of the usual air of greeting I saw a startled, terrified expression, a sort of look of shock, and simultaneously I saw this fellow who had been standing in the recess oppose Huey with a little black gun. This was right within a foot of me, so I threw my hands at him to grab him, just as he shot, and Murphy Roden—I don't know where he came from but I presume he had followed the Senator out into the hall from the inner office—anyway, at the same instant when I threw my hands and the shot was fired, Murphy Roden lunged and seized the gun and the man's hand in his left hand. This must have been at almost the very instant the shot was fired, for Murphy's hand kept the shell of the little automatic from ejecting, which is why the man whose body was later identified as that of Dr. Weiss could not fire another shot.

"It is hard to describe in sequence all the things that were happening in practically one and the same instant. As Murphy grappled with Weiss, the gesture I had made to push the man away was completed, and my hands pushed the two struggling men partly to the floor. Weiss had both hands around his gun, trying to fire again, and this time at Roden; and Roden, while holding his desperate clutch about the gun which was waving wildly this way and that, was trying to get his own gun from his shoulder holster, and I was still standing there with my hands outstretched from pushing them, when Elliott Coleman from quite a ways down the hall fired the second shot I heard that night, as well as two others.

"In that same instant of general confusion that boiled up I heard Huey give just one shout, a sort of hoot, and then he ran like a wild deer. I bent over to help Roden disarm Weiss, and twisted a muscle in my back so that for a moment I could not move in any direction. It was then I saw that one of Elliott Coleman's bullets had shot away Murphy Roden's wrist watch, but the next two hit Weiss. At the first one his whole body jerked convulsively—like this. At the second it jerked again in a great twitch as he sank into himself and slumped forward, face down, his head in the angle of the wall and his legs extended diagonally out into the corridor.

"It was not until after Weiss was dead that other body-guards came up and emptied their pistols into the fallen body. Meanwhile I caught a glimpse of other armed men, state police and bodyguards, charging from the [House chamber] end of the hall toward where the body was lying, and I caught one flash of my father wrestling around with some of them because he thought I was in trouble and he wanted to stop the shooting. I saw the crowd down there and I went into the other cross hall [the one in the direction of the Senate chamber] where there were stairs to the basement, and asked the girl at the telegraph desk which way Huey had gone, and she pointed down the stairs. . . ."

There is general agreement here that of the first two shots, by whomever fired, the first one penetrated Long's body, the second ripped Roden's watch from his wrist, and that the next two killed Dr. Weiss. The only discrepancy between the accounts of Murphy Roden and Justice Fournet is as to who fired these shots. According to Roden, the first two were fired by Weiss, the third by himself and the fourth by someone else, presumably Coleman. According to Justice Fournet, the first one was fired by Weiss, who never fired again; while the second shot, the one which according to both versions shot away Roden's wrist watch, was fired by Coleman, who there-after also fired the two shots that took Dr. Weiss's life.

How does Sheriff Coleman's account of what took place compare with these two? There is one marked point of difference. It involves a blow with the fist which no one else describes. Here, then, is that portion of Coleman's narrative of what took place:

". . . At this point a slight young fellow in a white linen suit stepped forward and stretched out his hand with a gun in it and pressed it against Huey's right side and fired. Everything happened very fast then, because the House had just adjourned, seemingly; anyway, people were coming out. I reached the young man about the same time Roden did, and hit him with my fist, knocking him down. He was trying to shoot and Murphy was grappling with him, so that he fell on top of Murphy when I hit him. I fired one shot. By that time Huey was gone, and I learned later he had gone down the stairs and had been taken to the hospital.

"The young man in the white linen suit, whom none of us knew at the time, was dead, and the gun was lying on the floor several inches from his hand. It was then that I saw why he had not fired again. A cartridge was jammed in the ejector. After that a lot of things happened, and there was a lot of shooting.

"They called me into the governor's office. Some fool had run in there, and Allen said to me: 'Coleman, I understand you hit that party. Huey isn't much hurt, he's just shot through the arm.' I said: 'The hell he is! The man couldn't have missed him. He shot him in the belly, right here.' Allen said: 'But they say you hit him and deflected the bullet.' And I said: 'I never hit him till after he shot.' All of this stuff about a bullet from one of the bodyguards is a lot of ——! Those boys all had .44s and .45s and if one of those bullets had gone through him it would have made a great big hole. Anybody knows that. Besides, when all the bodyguard shooting was going on, Huey was gone from that place and on his way downstairs."

This last is also borne out by Frampton, whose account of the actual shooting includes the following observations:

"While the conversation" (i.e., between Long and A. P. White about making sure that all Long supporters would be present at the early caucus and the morning House session) "was going on, this slight man I did not know but who had been leaning against a column in the angle of the marble wall, sort of sauntered over to him, and there was the sound of a shot, a small sound, a sort of pop. Huey grabbed his side and gave a sort of grunt, and I think he may have said 'I'm shot!' while running toward the stairs. He disappeared by the time Murphy Roden materialized out of somewhere—I never did see where he came from—and seized the man's hand. There were two shots and he crumpled forward, and fell with his head on his arm against the pillar where he had been standing, and his legs projected out into the hall. Huey had already disappeared around the corner and, as I learned later, down the stairway. The small automatic had slid out of Dr. Weiss's hand and lay about four inches from it on the floor by the time the other bodyguards came up, among them Messina and McQuiston, and emptied their guns into the prostrate figure."

Meanwhile Jimmie O'Connor, with Huey's Corona Belvedere cigars in the breast pocket of his coat, jumped up as he heard a sound, muffled by the heavy glass doors of the newly air-conditioned cafeteria, "like cannon crackers going off."

"I started to walk out," he recalls, "and as I opened the door I saw Huey reeling like this, with his arms extended, coming down those steps that were near the governor's office. He was all by himself, and I ran over to him and asked: 'What's the matter, Kingfish?' He spit in my face with blood as he gasped: 'I'm shot!' They put in the paper next day he said: 'Jimmie, my boy, I'm shot! Help me!' but he never said a damn word like that. All he said was 'I'm shot,' and he spit blood over me so that I thought he had been shot in the mouth.

"With that I grabbed him and I heard more shooting going on. They were still shooting at the fallen body of Dr. Weiss, as I found out later. But it shows how quickly it all happened. As fast as that. He had no blood on his clothes at all at that time, other than what he had spit out of his mouth.

"So I half carried and half dragged him outside to the driveway. They had a fellow out there with an old sort of a beat-up Ford automobile, and I said: 'Take me and this man over to the hospital.' It was an open-model car, not a sedan. Going over to the hospital Huey said not a word, just slumped and slid in my arms. When we got over there, I opened the car door and halfway got him out and got him on my shoulder, and whoever was in the car just blew. They were gone. Right by the entrance on the side they had a rolling table. I put him on that and rang the bell. One of the sisters came down and cried: 'Oh, oh! What is this?' and I said: 'The Senator.'

"She said: 'Wheel him into the elevator.' I did that. She operated the elevator and when we got out—I don't remember what floor it was—she and I wheeled him into the operating room, where an intern hurried over to us. Huey was wearing a cream-colored double-breasted suit, silky-looking, and I said to the intern: 'He's been shot in the mouth.' The intern pulled down the Senator's mouth, swabbed it out, and said: 'He's not shot there, that's just a little cut where he hit himself against something.' I suppose he stumbled up against the wall while reeling around the turns going down the stairs.

"Then the intern was beginning to open the Senator's coat when Dr. Vidrine popped in, and he and the intern opened the coat. There was very little blood on the shirt, and when they opened that and pulled up the undershirt we saw a very small hole right under the right nipple. . . . While his shirt and coat were being cut off, he asked the Sister to pray for him. 'Sister, pray for me,' he said, and she told him: 'Pray *with* me.'"

By this time frantic telephone calls to physicians in Baton Rouge and New Orleans, to Seymour Weiss and Earle Christenberry, to the Long family, to Adjutant General Fleming, and to a host of politicians had jammed the switchboards. Both the big buildings facing one another across the width of the old University Lake—the Sanitarium and the State House —were swarming hives of confused activity. In the hospital various officials and others in the top echelon of the Long organization were crowding the hallways around the wounded Senator's room, and later even the operating room itself, while the constant arrival of more and yet more cars clotted into an all but hopeless traffic snarl in the Sanitarium's small parking lot.

Others made their way to the capitol building as word of the shooting spread, but here General Louis F. Guerre, commandant of the Bureau of Identification, and Colonel E. P. Roy, chief of the highway police, acted promptly to restore some semblance of order. Part of the confusion stemmed from the fact that up to that very moment no one had been able to identify the body which later proved to be that of Dr. Weiss; almost everyone who asked to see if he might perhaps recognize the slight figure in the bloodstained white suit was admitted to the corridor where the corpse remained until Coroner Thomas Bird arrived. As described by Frampton——

"A number of people came around after the shooting stopped. Among them were Helen Gilkison, the *Item* and *Tribune* Baton Rouge correspondent and Colonel Roy. I remember that the Colonel took hold of the fallen man's head and lifted it so that the features were visible. He asked first me and then Helen if we knew him. We did not. I had never seen him before, as far as I knew then or know now.

"Then I suddenly remembered that George Coad in New Orleans, who was still on the phone line I had left open, must have heard the shooting and was likely going mad. So I went in and picked up the phone and told him Huey was shot, and the man who fired at him had been killed by the bodyguards, but that the body had not yet been identified, so he had better go with just that much for an extra.

"I then ran back out into the hall and found that Dr. Tom Bird, the coroner, was there. Colonel Roy and the state police were starting to clear the corridor of everyone: spectators, newspaper people, legislators, and all. But Dr. Bird deputized Helen as an assistant coroner, and she was permitted to stay. I then followed Huey's course down the stairs by the route I was told he had taken, and learned for the first time he really had been shot, because on the marble steps I saw a few drops of blood.

"I ran out the back door and was told he had been taken to the hospital by Jimmie O'Connor, so I ran around the end of the lake all the way from the capitol to Our Lady of the Lake Hospital, climbed the front steps, went up to the top floor, where Huey was lying on one of those surgical tables in the corridor outside of a room at the east end of the hallway.

"Right away I thought of Urban Maes and Jim Rives, and asked Colonel Roy, who had come there in the meantime, to get the airport lighted, as I would try to get Maes and Rives to fly up with Harry Williams. I put in calls for both of them and left messages about what had happened, and for them to get hold of Harry Williams and fly to Baton Rouge, where the airport had been lighted. . . . Actually, this had not yet been done, as I learned later. Colonel Roy could not raise any airport attendant, so he drove out there, kicked in a window, and turned on the lights himself."

By that time Dr. Maes and his associate, Dr. Rives, were already en route to Baton Rouge by automobile. They had been called at once by Seymour Weiss, who then jumped into his new Cadillac with Bob Maestri—the latter lived at the Roosevelt—and together they ruined the engine of the car by driving at top speed to Baton Rouge.

At that time no one yet had given out any reasonably

authoritative word as to whether Long was the victim of a major or minor injury; whether the prognosis was hopeful or a matter of doubt; whether his condition could be described as undetermined, satisfactory, or critical.

But so widespread was public interest in the Kingfish, who had challenged Roosevelt, and who only a month before had said the New Deal was at least cognizant of a plot to murder him, that newspapers in many distant cities lost no time in dispatching special correspondents and photographers to Baton Rouge to cover the day's top news story. The fight to save the Kingfish's life was just beginning.

*"He that cuts off twenty years
of life cuts off so many years
of fearing death."*

——SHAKESPEARE

Among the first of the Long hierarchs to reach the hospital to which Jimmie O'Connor had rushed the fallen Kingfish were Dr. Vidrine, Justice Fournet, and Acting Lieutenant Governor Noe. As a matter of fact, O'Connor had not yet left the capitol's porte-cochere when Fournet and Noe reached it.

"I heard Huey and Jimmie O'Connor talking before I saw them in the darkness there," Justice Fournet relates. "Jimmie asked: 'Where did he hit you?' and Huey said: 'Hell, man, take me to the hospital.' I reached them just as they got into the car of a man—his name was Starns, I think—and I tried to get into the car with them, but it was just a two-door affair, and I could not get in. By that time Jimmie Noe had come down, so he and I managed to get to the hospital in another of the cars around there. They had Huey sort of strapped to a wheeled table, an operating table, I suppose, by the time we got there and found out what floor he was on.

"Dr. Vidrine was there, and starting to take off some of the Senator's clothes; but I took out my pocket knife and said: 'Here, cut it off.' He slashed through the clothes and laid them back. I saw a very small bluish puncture on the right side of Huey's abdomen, and it was not bloody. And I saw Dr. Vidrine lift up the right side of Huey's back, but he did not lift it very far. Dr. Vidrine put us in a room with a nurse, then, and gave instructions to let no one else come in.

"Meanwhile other doctors were taking his blood pressure and pulse rate. Huey asked one of them what it was, and he told him. Naturally, I don't remember the figures, but I do remember Huey saying: 'That's bad, isn't it?' and Vidrine or one of the others"—[it was Dr. Cecil Lorio]—"answered him, saying: 'Well, not *too* bad, yet.' Vidrine asked him what doctors he wanted called, and he said Sanderson from Shreveport, and Maes and Rives from New Orleans. While they were waiting for their arrival, Joe Bates came in. He was allowed to come there so he could tell Huey who had shot him. He said it was a young doctor named Weiss.

"'What for?' Huey asked. 'I don't even know him.'

"'He's a fanatic about you,' Bates replied. 'But he is friendly with a lot of others in the administration.'"

Pending the arrival of surgeons from New Orleans, some semblance of order was being restored about the hospital. Highway motorcycle officers unsnarled the traffic jam in the Sanitarium's small parking lot, set up guarded barriers, and thereafter admitted to the grounds no one who did not have a special permit.

It was during this interlude, too, that Ty Campbell finally brought Murphy Roden from the capitol to the hospital for treatment.

"One of the interns washed my eyes out first," Roden remembers. "They were smarting and there must have been some powder residue in them. There were powder burns on the skin of my back, burns that had gone through my coat, my shirt, and my undershirt. These were cleaned and swabbed with antiseptic. But it was not until several weeks later, after a place on my back kept festering, that I went to my family doctor in Baton Rouge, and he finally removed a small fragment of the copper jacketing of a bullet, from where it had lodged just under the skin.

"After the interns finished with me, Ty went to the Istrouma Hotel and brought me back some clothes, and I changed in the hospital. After that we went back to the capitol with General Guerre, who took me to the office of the governor's executive counsel where General Ray Fleming, head of the National Guard, had set up his headquarters, and we talked nearly an hour or so, with me telling all I could recall. From there I went to my quarters and to bed."

When he returned to the capitol with Roden, General Guerre had the State House hallways cleared.

"Once I satisfied myself that the Senator had been taken to the hospital and was in the hands of physicians," he explains, "I gave orders to my men to clear the capitol's lower floor as quickly as possible, and allow no one else to come in without special authorization from me. I put officers in charge to see that the body of the assassin was not touched until the coroner got there. Even Dr. Bird did not know who the man was till they removed his wallet and saw his identification there."

Unaware of what had taken place in Baton Rouge, Earle Christenberry reached his New Orleans home shortly after 9:30, having driven in from the capitol without special haste. His neighbors, seeing the car turn into the Christenberry driveway, flung open a window and told him someone in Baton Rouge was trying to get in touch with him. His phone had not answered, whereupon the caller secured from the telephone company the number of the adjoining house, asking that when Earle arrived he be requested to call back immediately.

Then, adding a bit of news they had heard a short time earlier over the radio, they told him Huey Long had been shot.

Christenberry did not pause to call Baton Rouge. Without

leaving his car, he backed out of the driveway and headed for the capitol. He made but one stop en route. That was at Lousteau's combination sandwich counter and automobile agency, where the Airline Highway cut across the government's newly completed Bonnet Carre Spillway over a bridge a mile and an eighth long, spanning the dry channel through which the Mississippi River's flood waters could be diverted into Lake Pontchartrain. Final inspection of the structure had not yet been made; hence it was not open to general traffic. Wooden highway barriers blocked entry to it.

However, Christenberry directed the highway patrolman on duty there to open the barriers for him, since this would save at least six miles on the road to Baton Rouge. After ascertaining that Mrs. Long and the three children had not yet passed this point, he instructed the motorcycle man to remain on watch for their car, and open the barrier to let it pass over the bridge too.

Approximately seventy minutes after leaving his home, he parked at Our Lady of the Lake Sanitarium.

Earlier that afternoon, in New Orleans, General Ray Fleming, Adjutant General of Louisiana, had taken part at Jackson Barracks in a polo game between teams representing the 108th Cavalry and the famed Washington Artillery. During one of the late chuckers a hard-hit ball had banged against the General's left foot, inflicting an injury not in itself serious, but so painful that before retiring for the night he borrowed a pair of crutches from the post infirmary and secured a left shoe he could cut to accommodate the swelling which had followed the mishap.

"Hardly had I retired," he relates, "than I received a phone call from Governor Allen, who in a very excited voice said to me: 'Huey has been shot!' Realizing that I must have certain information to deal with such a situation, I demanded that the Governor stay on the telephone at least long enough to answer one question before I took action.

"The question was: 'Is this an action involving many persons or is it the act of just one individual?' This I had to know in order to determine what troops, if any, were needed to handle the situation.

"Governor Allen immediately informed me that it was the spontaneous action of just one individual. With this information in hand, I started almost at once for Baton Rouge. In a remarkably short time I reached the capitol, where I immediately set up headquarters in the office of the executive counsel. From then until about 2 A.M. I talked to a great many persons regarding events leading up to, during, and after the assassination.

"One of the reasons for this inquiry was that I had to make a decision as to whether or not we were faced with the necessity of dealing with an armed insurrection on the part of a considerable number of individuals."

Early that Sunday night Judge Leche, still inclined to make light of his conversation with Senator Long some hours before, was leaving Baptist Hospital, where his physician, Dr. Wilkes Knolle, had just changed the dressing of the airplane splint in which his left arm was immobilized.

"Our chauffeur was driving Tonnie [Mrs. Leche] and me home from the hospital," his account of the day's events continues, "and as we drew up in front of my house in Metairie I could hear the phone ring. I tossed my keys to the chauffeur and said: 'Hurry up and answer it, and tell whoever it is I'll be there as soon as I can work my way out of the car.' He did so, and I got out awkwardly, my left arm being held rigidly horizontal at shoulder height with the elbow bent, and when I got to the phone it was Abe Shushan telling me Huey had just been shot. I called out to the chauffeur not to leave, we were going to Baton Rouge right away, and I told Tonnie I would send the car back for her and she could come up the next day, if that seemed indicated.

"I went directly to the governor's office, and Oscar Allen was there, very nervous and visibly shaken. He was talking on the telephone and picked up a sheet of paper while holding the other hand over the mouthpiece, and said: 'This is what I am going to release to the press.' At the time I thought he said he had already released it. In brief, the statement said for everyone to remain calm, this had been merely the irresponsible act of one individual, and that it did not mean more than just one individual's crazed action.

"I tore the paper up and handed the pieces back to him, saying: 'Huey has been charging in Louisiana and in Washington that there was a plot on foot to kill him, and that he surrounded himself with bodyguards for that reason. He conducted a formal investigation into a murder plot with witnesses who said they had won their way into the confidence of the plotters, and named them, and carried on an investigation in New Orleans for days. . . . How in the world can you take it on yourself to proclaim officially that this was all twaddle, and that only one individual was responsible for what happened?'

"He said very excitedly: 'You're right, you're right, you're right!' I left, and was driven over to the hospital, but by that time the operation was either over or in progress, so I did not see Huey. I stayed in the hotel, and Tonnie joined me there the next day."

The operation was begun at 11:22 P.M., but Drs. Maes and Rives were not present. What happened is told by Dr. Rives in the following account:

"Dr. Maes had been called, I have forgotten by whom, and he was asked to fly to Baton Rouge as Huey Long had been shot; a chartered plane would be waiting for him at the New Orleans airport, and a highway car at the one in Baton Rouge. He asked me to go with him to assist him if he had surgery to do, and I told him there was no sense in flying to Baton Rouge, because I could drive him there in the time it would take to drive out to the New Orleans airport, and then, after the flight, from the Baton Rouge airfield to the hospital. This proved to be not right.

"We were in my car and I was driving. The road then ran beside the old O-K Interurban Line tracks, and just outside of Metairie an S-curve crossed the tracks, a black-top road with graveled shoulders. Just before we entered this S-curve another car, coming from the opposite direction, swept through it and put its bright lights right into my eyes. I was going about forty-five or fifty. I was not racing, in other words, but I got my right wheel into the loose gravel of the shoulder, and ended up skidding completely around and facing back in the direction of New Orleans on the old gravel road beyond the S-curve.

"My differential housing was caught on the high center of this old gravel road, with only one rear wheel on the ground. We did no damage to the car, but with only one wheel on the ground, a car is helpless. We finally flagged someone driving back toward New Orleans and asked him to send a wrecker to pull us back on the road. Actually they sent only a truck, but it took us off the high center and then we went on. I should say we lost not more than half an hour, but I think we would not have reached Baton Rouge until after the operation even if we had not met with this accident.

"We did not have permission to use the completed but not yet opened Airline Highway beyond Kenner, so I took the old River Road. As we finally drove into Baton Rouge, there wasn't a soul in sight, aside from a policeman or two. No one was abroad on the streets; lights in the houses, yes, but no people or cars on the streets. To outward appearances, it was the most deserted community I ever saw, and going to Our Lady of the Lake Sanitarium we had to drive right through the center of town.

"At the hospital we were met by highway police, identified ourselves, which was required, and then we were conducted to the entrance where someone else took us up to the ward where Huey had been placed. . . ."

Word of the shooting of Huey Long had spread through the capitol's corridors and offices with almost explosive speed. The minute she heard the report, Lucille May Grace (Mrs. Fred Dent in private life), Register of the State Land Office, tried to telephone Dr. Clarence Lorio, who, though not Senator Long's physician, was one of his closest friends in the Baton Rouge area. Mrs. Dent (since deceased) was devoted to Huey Long, for he had supported her father for re-election to the office of Land Register, a post which he held for more than thirty years. Upon her father's death Long appointed her to serve in Mr. Grace's stead for the unexpired balance of his term, since she had been his principal assistant almost from the very day she was graduated from Louisiana State University.

Since she had retained, and even added to, her father's tremendous personal following among the voters, Huey decided at the end of her term of office in 1932 to put her name on the Allen slate, which would carry his imprimatur as the "Complete-the-Work" ticket. Hoping to induce Long to rescind this decision, one or another of the rival aspirants spread a completely baseless rumor to the effect that Mrs. Dent's ancestry was tainted with a touch of Negro blood.

Huey Long's almost obsessive response to this sort of aspersion was a matter of common knowledge; it is only because what ensued may have some bearing on the motive behind the assassination that this particular incident is worth giving in some detail.

Though he had already consented to put the name of Lucille May Grace on the slate that would carry his endorsement, he lost no time in retracting this agreement, and made it crystal clear forthwith that unless she could show to his complete satisfaction that the rumor which had gained considerable circulation was without even the semblance of a foundation, he would place another's name on the ticket for the position she, and before her her father, had held.

Miss Grace, the niece of an Iberville parish priest, enlisted the latter's aid and that of the late John X. Wegmann, a universally respected New Orleans insurance man and perhaps the foremost Catholic layman in Louisiana at the time. Thus birth and baptismal records going back for generations along the Grace family tree were produced, and they conclusively demonstrated the utter falsity of the canard. Satisfied, Long restored her name at once to his personally approved "Complete-the-Work" ticket of candidates, headed by the name of Oscar K. Allen for governor.

Miss Grace (she did not become Mrs. Dent until a year later) had attended Louisiana State University with both Clarence and Cecil Lorio, and knew how close the former's friendship with Senator Long was. She began at once to call him, but he was not at his farm in nearby Pointe Coupee parish, and the telephone at his Baton Rouge residence was apparently out of order. So she called his brother, Dr. Cecil Lorio.

"Suppose you let me tell the whole story, exactly as I recall it," the latter began, when asked about his recollections of what took place in the operating room of Our Lady of the Lake Sanitarium when Huey Long was admitted there as a patient that September night. Dr. Cecil Lorio and Dr. Walter

Cook were, at the time of this inquiry, the only surviving physicians who were present throughout all the ensuing surgical procedure.

"When she failed to reach my brother Clarence," Dr. Lorio continued, "Lucille May Grace called me at my home, and I left at once for Our Lady of the Lake Sanitarium. Huey's clothing had been removed by the time I got there, and he was in bed in his room at the east end of the third-floor corridor. He was fully conscious and we talked quietly from time to time during the next hour. He was particularly distressed by the thought that he might now be unable to carry out his plan to screen students for L.S.U., so as to make it possible for all exceptionally bright high-school graduates, however needy their families, to receive the advantages of college education.

"I took his blood pressure and pulse every fifteen minutes; he had evidently learned something about the significance of this, for when he asked me what the readings were, and I told him his pulse rate was getting faster and his blood pressure was dropping a bit, he said: 'That's not good, is it?' and I answered him by saying: 'No, but it isn't too bad yet, either.' 'It means there's an internal hemorrhage?' he then asked. I said he was probably hemorrhaging some, but that the relation between blood pressure and pulse rate was one that could also be attributed to shock. He was very curious about who had shot him, saying it was someone he had never seen before.

"He had visibly a small blue puncture on the right side of his abdomen, and another on the right side of his back where the bullet emerged. Both were very small. But it was obvious some emergency surgery would have to be performed sooner or later. I was told that Dr. Sanderson had been summoned from Shreveport, and that Drs. Urban Maes and James Rives were already en route from New Orleans. Dr. Maes had been appointed to the chair of surgery at L.S.U.'s new medical college, of which Dr. Vidrine, also present in Baton Rouge at the time, was dean, along with his position as superintendent of Charity Hospital. He was in general charge of the patient's case. At some point in the proceedings word was brought to us that a motoring accident had forced Dr. Rives's car off the road, and that they would be delayed some time by the difficulty of securing service at that time of night to have their car dragged back to the highway. When informed of this, Dr. Vidrine decided not to wait any longer."

Huey's very close friends, Seymour Weiss and Conservation Commissioner Robert Maestri, had reached Baton Rouge some time prior to this. It is Mr. Weiss's clear recollection that the decision to wait no longer before performing an emergency operation was reached "by all of us" before word was received of the mischance encountered by Drs. Maes and Rives.

"As I recall the circumstances," Seymour Weiss says, "Huey's condition was getting worse by the minute. Dr. Vidrine insisted that any further delay was progressively lessening the Senator's chances. The other physicians present agreed that the outlook was not hopeful. Vidrine was the physician in charge and the rest of us were laymen. The time came when we either had to agree to let the operation be performed at once, or take upon ourselves the risk of endangering the man's life. Mrs. Long and the children had not yet reached Baton Rouge, but in view of the medical opinions, the rest of us—all being individuals who were close to Huey —were just about unanimous in agreeing that the doctors should proceed."

Amid the almost inconceivable confusion in and out of the hospital, one person seems to have kept her head, and that was Miss Mary Ann Woods, now Mrs. Arthur Champagne, the supervisor of nurses. Assigning floor nurses and trainees to duties so as to make the best possible disposition of available personnel, she set out to provide four special attendants for the critically injured Senator, two to serve at night and two by day.

The first one she called from the register was Theoda Carriere, who responded at once, even though she had just come off a twelve-hour tour of duty. The other three were Loretta Meade, Helen Selassie, and Mrs. Hamilton Baudin. Miss Carriere was one of the first to reach the hospital, as she lived nearby; and since by that time Senator Long had been taken from his third-floor sickroom to the operating theater on the floor above, she scrubbed up at once and reported for duty there.

According to her recollection, Dr. Cook was working on the patient, who was anesthetized by the time she arrived. Being short of stature, she had difficulty in seeing the operating table, and therefore placed a stool so that, by standing on it, she could look over the shoulders of those surrounding the patient.

Dr. Cook said to her: "This is a gunshot wound; get me some antitetanus serum." Miss Carriere left the room for the pharmacy section downstairs where such supplies were stored, and when she returned with the desired serum, and gave it to Dr. Cook, Dr. Vidrine was just entering the operating room.

"Dr. Cook looked up," she relates, "and said: 'Well, my relief has arrived,' and left the operating room. Dr. Ben Chamberlain assisted Dr. Vidrine during the balance of the operation."

In this respect Miss Carriere's recollections are in direct conflict with those of every physician who was present, and with the operation report attached to the hospital chart, as well as with the statement of Dr. Cook himself, when he testified later that he assisted at the operation.

As operating procedure was begun in the Sanitarium, neighbors of Dr. Clarence Lorio, seeing his car parked in front of his home, and realizing that under normal circumstances he of all men would have been at the hospital with his gravely wounded friend, managed to rouse him.

"I had been working for thirteen hours straight," he explained subsequently, "and I was bone tired. When I got home I not only went to bed, but took the telephone off the hook so as not to be disturbed. I had come to the point where I simply had to rest. Naturally, when some of my neighbors woke me and told me what had happened, I lost no time in dressing and rushing off to the Sanitarium, but the operation was already under way when I got there.

"Let me say this about Arthur Vidrine: that man faced one of the toughest decisions that night anybody ever confronted. If he sat idly by, waiting for someone else to take over the case, while Huey bled to death, his associates and Huey's friends would never forgive him, and he would never forgive himself, either. On the other hand, if he performed an emergency operation, and it was discovered later that the critically wounded patient would have had a better chance for recovery if some other procedure had been followed, he would still be blamed for a great man's death. No one could confront a more harrowing choice."

On the other hand, it can be taken for granted that Arthur Vidrine must at least momentarily have entertained the thought of the rewards and renown that would be his portion if by timely, courageous, and skillful surgery he, rather than others, saved the life of the Kingfish of Louisiana. Be that as it may, the decision to operate at once was made; when it was submitted to Senator Long, he concurred in it; in fact, according to a monograph by Dr. Frank L. Loria of New Orleans, Huey himself said: "Come on, let's go be operated upon."

Dr. Cecil Lorio described the incident more prosaically in the following terms:

"Someone told him that it had been decided to operate and that Dr. Vidrine would perform the operation if Huey had no objection. He indicated that he was willing for this to be done. Dr. Vidrine selected Dr. William Cook to assist him, and Dr. Henry McKeown as the anesthetist. It was this latter choice that brought me back into the operating room and kept me there, for I am a pediatrician, not a surgeon.

"Baton Rouge—in fact, all Louisiana—was bitterly divided into Long and anti-Long factions at this time. One of the most violently partisan anti-Long individuals in all Baton Rouge was Henry McKeown. He really hated Huey, though he had many friends among the people who were close to the Senator.

"Only two or three nights earlier, he and I were both sitting in at a poker game in the Elks' Club, when someone said something or other about Long—probably something in connection with the special session of the legislature that might be called any day. Dr. McKeown said in jest, the way any person might in the course of a sociable card game: 'If ever he has to have an operation, they better not let me give the anesthetic, for I'll guarantee he'd never get off that table.' Let me say again, and with emphasis, that this was not a threat, but a jest, something to underscore the man's uncompromising anti-Long partisanship.

"Naturally, when within a matter of days he actually was summoned to serve as anesthetist for an operation to be performed on Huey Long, he demurred. He pointed out that Huey was a bad operative risk in any case, and for all anyone knew to the contrary, might already be dying from a wound which was in itself mortal. 'If the man dies during the operation,' Dr. McKeown pointed out, 'many of those who have heard me pop off about him might actually think I killed him.' No one who knew Henry McKeown, of course, would think any such thing. Finally he agreed to serve, provided I watched and checked every move he made.

"I told him I would do so, but while I looked now and then across the operating table to its head, where he was standing, and saw what he was doing, I really paid no attention to it, nor did he stop to see whether or not I was checking on him.

"Later, while the operation was in progress, Dr. Clarence Lorio, my brother, came in and stood beside Dr. McKeown to the end of the operation. On the side of the table at Huey's left stood Dr. Vidrine. Opposite him was his assistant, Dr. Cook. Beside Dr. Vidrine at his left, I stood, handing him instruments and materials as he called for them. As I said, I am not a surgeon, but a pediatrician.

"The operating room was a strange sight. All sorts of people, mostly politicians, I assume, had crowded into the small room. It was not an amphitheater, and they ranged themselves all along the walls, not even being suited up. As Mother Henrietta, the head of the hospital, said later, after she had vainly tried to keep all who were not physicians or properly gowned out of the operating chamber, it was anything but normal surgical procedure."

It is indeed a pity the original chart, such as it was, could not have been preserved. But as in the case of most hospitals, the time came when the absolute limit of storage capacity was exhausted, and the charts on file were microfilmed. In making these microfilms it was customary in many hospitals not to include the nurses' bedside notes in the filmed record. Hence these do not appear in the film of the chart of Huey Long at Lady of the Lake.

But even what does remain is fragmentary, and in many cases unsigned. As Dr. Rives observed many years later: "The situation that night, even after I arrived, which was after the operation was completed and Huey was back in his room,

could only be described as chaotic. Several physicians seemed
to be on hand, and in the case of a critically injured patient,
when no one of the attending doctors is actually in command
and giving the orders to the crew of which he is the captain
. . . well, all I can say is that even during the four hours or
so when I was there between about 1 A.M. and the time I
started back for New Orleans which I reached at daybreak,
the situation was nothing short of chaotic."

A transcript of the microfilm was made by Dr. Chester A.
Williams, the present coroner of East Baton Rouge parish.
According to this document, the admitting note, set down on
a plain sheet of paper, is not even signed; obviously the last
two lines were added by someone else after the operation was
concluded. It is preceded on the record by a standard summary
form which reads:

Hospital No. 24179. Sen. Huey P. Long, 42 yr.w.m.
Admitted Sept. 8, 1935, to Dr. Vidrine.
Diagnosis: Shot wound abdomen, perforation of colon,
          Room 325.
Died Sept. 10, 1935.

The unsigned "admitting note" on its plain sheet of paper,
which follows the foregoing summary, reads:
"Pt. admitted to O.R. at 9:30 P.M. Dr. Vidrine present.
Exam made by Dr. Vidrine shows wound under ribs rt. side,
clothes and body with blood. Pulse volume weak and faint.
Fully conscious, very nervous. Given caffeine and sodium
benzoate 2 cc by hypo. Dr. Cook present. Put to bed in 314
at 9:45 P.M. Foot of bed elevated. M.S. gr. ⅙ by hypo for
pain. Asked for ice continuously. Dr. Cecil Lorio present.
External heat, Pt. in cold sweat. After consultation, patient
to O.R. at 11:20, pulse weak and fast, still asks for ice."

Then follow the words, obviously added after the operation:

"Dr. Vidrine, C. A. Lorio, Cecil and Dr. Cook present, and put to bed in 325 at 12:40 A.M. Foot of bed elevated."

The Operating Room record of the chart reads:

Surgeon: Dr. Vidrine.

Anesthetist: Dr. McKeown.

Assistants: Dr. Cook, Dr. C. A. Lorio, Dr. C. Lorio.

Anesthesia: N₂O started at 10:51 P.M. ended 12:14 A.M.
Pulse during anesthesia 104–114

Operation begun 11:22 P.M., ended 12:25 A.M.

What was done: Perforation—2—Transfer [sic!] colon.
[Signature not decipherable]

In the monograph previously referred to, Dr. Loria of New Orleans compiled a more detailed technical description of the surgical procedure. This was published in 1948 by the *International Abstracts of Surgery* (Volume 87) as a treatise dealing with 31,751 cases of abdominal gunshot wounds admitted to Charity Hospital during the first forty-two years of the present century. Dr. Loria appended to it a series of reports on notable personages in American history who had succumbed to such wounds, including President Garfield, President McKinley, and Senator Long. Referring to the Senator's case, he wrote in part:

"The bullet which struck Senator Long entered just below the border of the right ribs anteriorly, somewhat lateral to the mid-clavicular line. The missile perforated the victim's body, making its exit just below the ribs on the right side posteriorly and to the inner side of the midscapular line, not far from the midline of the back.

". . . At the hospital, arrangements were made for an emergency laparotomy with Vidrine in charge. . . . Under ether anesthesia the abdomen was opened by an upper right rectus muscle splitting incision. Very little blood was found in the peritoneal cavity. The liver, gall bladder and stomach were

free of injury. A small hematoma, about the size of a silver
dollar, was found in the mesentery of the small intestine. The
only intra-peritoneal damage found was a 'small' perforation
of the hepatic flexure, which accounted for a slight amount
of soiling of the peritoneum. Both the wounds of entry and
of exit in the colon were sutured and further spillage stopped.
The abdomen was closed in layers as usual."

About one o'clock that morning Drs. Maes and Rives arrived, and somewhat later Dr. Russell Stone, another noted
New Orleans surgeon. None of these saw any part of the
operative procedure, all surgery having been completed before their arrival. But a sharp difference of opinion between
Dr. Vidrine and Dr. Stone was followed by the latter's prompt
return to New Orleans without so much as looking at the
patient. Dr. Stone told some of his New Orleans associates
and close friends that Vidrine had given him the details of
the abdominal operation and had also said that the kidney
was injured and was hemorrhaging.

"Did you see the kidney?" he asked Vidrine, and added
that the latter replied: "No, but I felt it." An acrimonious
interchange followed and at its climax Vidrine said something to the general effect of "Well, go on in and examine
him for yourself." Stone replied: "Not I. This isn't my case
and he isn't my patient. Good night." Thereupon he returned
at once to New Orleans.

Dr. Rives's account of his experiences clearly illustrates on
what he based his opinion that the procedure was "chaotic."

"Dr. Maes and I were taken into a room next to the one
Huey was in," he related, "and there I stopped. Dr. Maes was
taken on into the patient's room, while I got off into a corner,
making myself inconspicuous. At this time there was still no
suggestion that anyone but Dr. Weiss had shot or even could
have shot Huey Long. Meanwhile, people were going in and
out of the sickroom, apparently at will. I did not know many

of them, and certainly most of them were not physicians. Finally someone, and I think it was Abe Shushan, asked me had I been in the room where Huey was, and I said no, I was only there to assist Dr. Maes in the event there was any surgery he had to perform. He said: 'In something like this we want the benefit of every doctor's advice,' and led me in there.

"I did not see the wound of entrance, and I was told by one of the nuns or one of the nurses that the wound of entrance was beneath the clean dressing on his belly; and from the location of this dressing it was clear to me that there was a good chance the bullet might have hit a kidney.

"I asked the nurses if there were any blood in his urine. That was the only contribution I could make. Whoever it was, she said she did not know. I said that if they did not know, he ought to be catheterized at once. Later that night, some time before I left for New Orleans, I was told he had been catheterized and that there was blood in his urine. That was an absolute indication of injury to the kidney. It was not necessarily a critical injury, or a hemorrhage that would not stop. But it did mean that there was an injury, and that if hemorrhage continued, that was the place to look for it."

Dr. Maes said there would be no further surgery, and hence while he would stay through the day, Monday, there would be no need for Dr. Rives to do so. The latter thereupon drove back to New Orleans.

According to Dr. Loria's monograph, the "postoperative course of the case continued steadily on the downgrade. Evidence of shock and hemorrhage appeared to become steadily worse . . . the urine was found to contain much blood. At this time [Dr. Russell] Stone's opinion was that another operation to arrest the kidney hemorrhage would certainly prove fatal. . . ."

Whether it was Dr. Rives or Dr. Stone who first suggested catheterization is immaterial. The fact remains that until one or the other of these physicians, neither of whom was directly connected with the case, proposed this procedure, nothing of the sort seems to have been done; according to the progress notes on the microfilm chart, it was not done until 6:45 A.M., almost nine hours after the shooting, and six hours after the emergency operation had precluded the possibility of further surgery. Even after it was discovered that the kidney hemorrhage was massive and continuing, medical opinion was unanimous on the point that additional surgery would unquestionably prove fatal.

Control of such hemorrhage involved removal of the injured kidney, in order to tie off the vessels supplying it with blood. This in turn would mean the cutting of ribs to make room for the requisite mechanics of kidney removal. Such an operation on a patient already in shock from a bullet wound and from the major abdominal surgery which followed, would, it was agreed by all, inevitably bring about the patient's death. All that remained was to hope for a miracle— and none manifested itself. In the words of Dr. Cecil Lorio:

"The patient never really recovered consciousness. He was in shock, and under sedation, until he died. As the day [Monday] wore on, and Huey's blood pressure continued to fall, a transfusion was ordered. It may have been earlier that the transfusion was given. The hospital records would show."

Unfortunately, the hospital record shows only one transfusion, given at 8:15 Monday night, nearly twenty-four hours after the shooting. However, it must be borne in mind that in those days, long before blood and plasma banks had been established as standard hospital facilities, transfusions were by no means the routine procedure they are today. In the case of Huey Long, a chart note signed by Dr. Roy Theriot records the fact that five hundred cubic centimeters of citrated blood were given, that before transfusion approximately three hundred cubic centimeters of normal saline solution were given intravenously at a time when the pulse was very thready, and that the transfusion was followed by a continuous intravenous drip of glucose in normal saline. Even after this the patient's blood pressure was only 114 over 84, while the pulse rate was still a frightening "170-plus."

Almost as soon as Senator Long had been brought to the hospital, volunteer blood donors were typed, and their blood cross-matched with that of the patient. According to the laboratory report incorporated in the hospital chart, J. A. Vitiano, Eddie Knoblock, Colonel Rougon, J. R. Pollett, M. E. Bird, George Castigliola, and Paul Voitier were marked "incompatible"; C. J. Campbell, John Kirsch, "no name," Joe Bates, Senator Noe, Bill Melton, and a Mr. Walker were found to be compatible. In addition, "no name," Bates, Noe, and Melton were also marked with an "O.K."

Senator Noe was the first and apparently only donor, and it is my recollection that we met in the Heidelberg Hotel elevator Monday night when he told me he had "just given blood to Huey." Mrs. Noe was with him at the time, said she was sure Senator Long would recover, and expressed the hope that future installments of the *Saturday Evening Post's* biographical portrait would "do him proud."

A little after two o'clock that afternoon Dr. Maes had prescribed a rectal instillation of laudanum, aspirin, brandy, and normal saline solution. Once this was given, the chart notes: "Resp. less labored, less cyanosis, P 148 Temp. 103-⅘ axilla. Quieter." During the handling that was incident to the instillation, Senator Long awoke and asked Dr. Maes whether he would be able to take the stump in the approaching campaigns. "It's a little early to tell, yet," the physician replied. As before, the patient lapsed into drugged slumber the moment the handling that had roused him came to an end.

As concerns the one transfusion recorded on the hospital chart, Dr. Cecil Lorio reports:

"I recall clearly the fact that the young physician who was to give the transfusion was so nervous, and his hands were shaking so, that he was having difficulty placing the needle in the vein that was to receive the blood; and my brother Clarence said to me, knowing that I frequently gave transfusions to children: 'Dr. Cecil, haven't you your equipment here so that you might assist in transfusing the Senator?' I said I had, and of course to me, accustomed to performing this with the small veins of children, it was child's play to place the needle in the large vein of a man. A number of volunteers—everybody wanted to volunteer—had already been typed, and one of those whose blood matched was State Senator James A. Noe. He was the first donor.

"But as the day wore on it became evident that the patient was losing blood about as fast as we were transfusing it into him, and while there were no external evidences of bleeding, the conclusion was that he must be hemorrhaging from the apex of the right kidney. So Dr. T. Jorda Kahle of New Orleans [head of the urology department of Louisiana State University's College of Medicine] was sent for. He got to Baton Rouge Monday night and thrust a needle just under the skin of the kidney region and drew out a syringeful of blood. That made it evident the Senator's case was hopeless, barring a miracle. The only way to stop such a hemorrhage would have been to remove the kidney, and that would certainly have killed him.

"At the end, the dying man threshed wildly about the oxygen tent that had been put over him. A little after four in the morning his breathing stopped."

Mrs. Long and the three children—Rose, Russell, and Palmer—did not reach Baton Rouge until after the operation was over, in spite of the fact that the Airline's new bridge across the Bonnet Carre Spillway was opened to the passage

of their car, thanks to Earle Christenberry's directions to the
highway guards at Lousteau's. Since the Senator was never
really conscious after he left the operating room, the members
of his family had little or no communion with the man who
to them was not merely a public figure, but husband and
father.

They were given rooms directly across the hall from the
one in which physicians strove unremittingly to save Huey
Long's life. He had not been a very devoted family man. He
was away from home too much in the pursuit of objectives
it seemed impossible for him to share with the Rose McConnell he had met when he was a brash young door-to-door
salesman of Cottolene.

Those days were now so long in the past, the happy days
of shared trial when every penny had to be stretched to the
uttermost. Success had come so quickly—the big ornate home
in Shreveport, the new Executive Mansion at Baton Rouge of
which Rose had been the first chatelaine, the elaborate residence on Audubon Boulevard, the days of triumph and re-
joicing that followed the effort to impeach him. . . .

All of it was now slipping away forever, while Huey Long's
blood seeped slowly but relentlessly out of his body, with no
possibility short of a miracle of halting its ebb as some physician, now forever anonymous, made on his hospital chart a
final entry to the effect that even "the oxygen tent discon-
tinued as pt. grew very restless under it—delusions of photographers, etc."

Once hope for the patient had been abandoned, it was Seymour Weiss who was the nuncio bringing to the members of
Huey's family, in the room across the hall, tidings of great
grief. Himself emotionally shaken to the depths of his being,
he told Mrs. Long and the three children as gently as possible
that the end was very near. They followed him across the
hall to the bed where the dying man, barely conscious, was

drawing in and expelling shallow, noisy breaths. He made no effort to speak; but as each of the four laid a hand on the bed beside him, he managed weakly to pat it in a final, caressing gesture of farewell.

They returned to their room to await the end. Seymour Weiss accompanied them, giving voice to whatever comforting phrases he could muster, and then returned to the sickroom. One vital point remained to be cleared up.

"Huey, Huey, can you hear me?" he asked.

There was a faint stir of response.

"Huey, you are seriously hurt. Everything that can be done to help you is being done, but no one can ever say how such things will turn out. Now is the time to tell me where you put the papers and things that you took out of the bank vault. Where did you put them? Tell me where they are, Huey. Please don't wait any longer."

Thus the final thoughts he carried with him out of his life concerned a political campaign, his campaign for the presidency of the United States. Hardly audible was the faint breath that whispered:

"Later—I'll—tell—you—later. . . ."

They were his last words. The secret of what became of the affidavits, the other documents, and the campaign funds that were to provision his presidential race was one he took with him to an elaborate tomb newly constructed in the very center of the landscaped park around the capitol he had built for Louisiana.

> "*And this was all the harvest*
> *that I reap'd—I came like*
> *water and like wind I go.*"
> ——THE RUBÁIYÁT

A few hours after Huey Long had breathed his last, Dr. Weiss was buried with requiem services at St. Joseph's Church, where he and Yvonne had gone to Mass only three days before. John M. Parker and J. Y. Sanders, Sr., two former governors prominent among leaders of the political and personal opposition to the Kingfish regime, attended the funeral, and were bitterly assailed by Long partisans for doing so. Dr. McKeown, the anesthetist during the emergency operation performed by Dr. Vidrine, was one of the pallbearers.

Yvonne's uncle, Dr. Pavy, a member of the House of Representatives, had been delegated by the Weiss family to act as their spokesman in meeting with reporters who had swarmed into Baton Rouge from near and far. It should be noted that at this time no one had as yet voiced the slightest doubt about Dr. Weiss having fired the shot that ended Long's reign. Only the question of motive was the subject for argument and dispute.

"There was absolutely nothing premeditated about what Carl did," Dr. Pavy told newsmen gathered at the little cottage he shared with Judge Philip Gilbert when in Baton Rouge. "On Sunday, while his parents sat on the beach of their camp with their baby grandchild, Carl and Yvonne sported about the water. When he returned home, he bade his wife an affectionate good-by, as he left about 7 P.M. for a professional call. He even phoned the Lady of the Lake Sanitarium to make an appointment for an operation Monday morning.

"He was an earnest lad, and lived for humanity, but he was sorely distressed about the suppressive form of government he felt existed in Louisiana. He never talked much about it, and he certainly never confided to his family or anyone else any plan to kill Long. Our only explanation for his action is that this suppressive type of rule preyed on his mind until it unhinged, and he suddenly felt himself a martyr, giving his life to the people of Louisiana. He must have felt that way, else how could he have left the wife and baby that he loved above everything?"

To a question as to whether the gerrymander that would oust his wife's father from the honorable office he had held for so many years could have prompted the decision to shoot Long, Dr. Pavy replied:

"In the first place, none of us would kill anyone over such a matter as the loss of a public office. It is my understanding that while the bill aimed at my brother's judgeship was discussed at the Weiss's dinner table Sunday, it was treated lightly rather than otherwise."

The legislature of which Dr. Pavy was a member had remained in session. "We're going to pass every one of ol' Huey's bills the same as if he was still here with us," was the majority watchword. In addition to these, the members also adopted a concurrent resolution authorizing the fallen leader's interment in the capitol grounds, and the construction there of a proper tomb to receive the great bronze casket, this to be topped by a monument later. They also adopted a concurrent resolution "recognizing and commending and according due recognition" to the valued services and help of the

Senator's bodyguards, mentioning by name specifically George McQuiston, assistant superintendent of the state police, Warden Louis Jones of the state penitentiary, and officers Murphy Roden, Theophile Landry, Paul Voitier, and Joe Messina.

During one of the interludes when the House was in session, I took occasion to go to Dr. Pavy's desk and ask whether he had reached any conclusion as to Dr. Weiss's motive other than the one he had mentioned on the previous Monday. I had heard vague reports that it was felt in some quarters Huey Long was planning to revive an old racial campaign canard against Judge Pavy. This was the allegation made in 1908 by the then Sheriff Swords to the effect that one of the Judge's relatives-in-law had an ancestor of other than purely Caucasian blood.

The old slur had long since been forgotten by most persons, since it dated back to 1907–8. In that era, though the quadroon ball had long since lapsed from the quasi recognition once accorded it, Northern magazines still published muckraking articles about miscegenation in the South. On the other hand, memories of relatively recent carpetbag evils were so vivid that the "taint of the tarbrush" was fatal to any political aspirant. Thus the fact that in spite of Sheriff Swords's allegations in a milieu of that sort, Judge Pavy was not only elected, but re-elected for five or six consecutive terms, testifies eloquently to the universal disbelief this imputation encountered.

Naturally, I did not spell all this out to Dr. Pavy. I merely made a casual reference to the general spread of all sorts of rumors about Dr. Weiss's motives, and asked whether he had any information on this score other than what he had told us on the morning after the shooting.

"I tell you again," he replied with profound conviction, "that this was an act of pure patriotism on Carl's part. He was ready to lay down his life to save his state, and perhaps this entire nation, from the sort of dictatorship which he felt Long had imposed on Louisiana."

None the less, in many minds—my own, for one—the feeling that there might be some substance to the racial motive would not down. Many Louisianians, for example, well knew that in his weekly, *American Progress,* Long never referred to the scion of a certain socially prominent family as anything but "Kinky" Soandso.

Even more recent in public memory was his insistent conjunction of Dudley LeBlanc with Negro officers in his "Coffin Club," the outlawed burial-insurance society. Moreover, the knowledge that a derogatory allegation was untrue never deterred Huey Long from trumpeting it forth at least by innuendo on every stump during a political campaign. For example, an office seeker opposing the candidacy of a man Long had endorsed was in the business of installing coin-activated devices for jukeboxes and an early type of vending machine, but Long never referred to him in his tirades as anything but Slot Machine Soandso.

Amid a fog of conflicting rumors and surmises, the first note of doubt that Carl Weiss, Jr., had even tried to kill Senator Long was sounded by the young physician's father, in a statement he made at an inquest into the circumstances of his son's death. Such as it was, this probe was conducted by District Attorney John Fred Odom, one of the leaders of the Square Deal Movement. It developed little more than one possible explanation of the contusion, abrasion, or cut visible on Long's lower lip when he reached the hospital.

"Was Senator Long bleeding from the mouth?" District Attorney Odom asked Dr. William A. Cook, after the latter stated that he had assisted Dr. Vidrine in the emergency operation on the mortally wounded patient.

"Dr. Henry McKeown, who was administering the anesthetic," responded Dr. Cook, "called my attention to an abrasion on Senator Long's lower lip. It was an abrasion or brush burn. When it was wiped with an antiseptic, it oozed a little."

"Did it appear to be a fresh abrasion?"

"Yes."

Attorney General Porterie, a pro-Long leader, asked Dr. Cook:

"A man having been shot as Senator Long was, and making his way down four winding flights of stairs, could perhaps have struck against an angle of marble or iron?"

"Any contusion or trauma could have caused such a bruise," was Dr. Cook's reply.

Only one new development of any potential significance was brought out by the inquiry. Sheriff Coleman testified that he struck twice with his fist before firing on Weiss and that "the first time I missed him and struck someone else, but the second time I hit him and knocked him down when Roden was grappling with him." Conceivably, the "someone else" of the first blow could have been Huey Long, although none of the other eyewitnesses mention such a blow. As for the remainder of the investigation, only one brief moment of emotional tension marked its course. That was when the Rev. Gerald L. K. Smith, a paid organizer of the Share-Our-Wealth movement, took the stand. He had been dropping hints here and there indicating his entire readiness to take over the Huey Long movement as its new leader. The moment he reached the witness stand he burst out dramatically to the effect that "my leader whom I worshiped has been killed. He was my hero. I respect this court, but I do not respect the district attorney, who was one of the co-plotters of this assassination, and I shall refuse to answer any questions put by him."

Mr. Odom said he had no questions to ask, adding: "I care nothing about him or his statements, but merely wish to state that whoever says I plotted to kill Huey Long is a willful, malicious, and deliberate liar."

Neither on this occasion, eight days after the event, nor for a long time thereafter did anyone deny, or offer to deny, that Carl Weiss had entered the capitol armed with a pistol and had fired it at Senator Long. Even the bitter-enders among Long's political foes came up with nothing more in the way of exoneration for the young physician than the suggestion that there had been two bullets, and that the second one, a wild shot or a ricochet from the gun of one of the bodyguards during the furious fusillade which followed the initial shot, had inflicted the wound that proved mortal.

True, Carl Weiss's father, testifying at the inquest, had expressed the opinion that his son was "too superbly happy with his wife and child, and too much in love with them to want to end his life after such a murder." But this was generally accepted as a natural expression of paternal love and grief, and therefore not to be taken as refuting the uncontradicted testimony of eyewitnesses and physicians.

The inquest conducted by Coroner Tom Bird into the death of Huey Long occupied only a few minutes. The family had refused to authorize a necropsy, the results of which might well have confirmed or silenced proponents of the two-bullet theory. These still emphasize the fact that no small-caliber bullet was ever found among the projectiles picked up from the floor of the corridor where the shooting occurred. They argue that if a small-caliber bullet were found to be still in Huey's body, the wound of exit must necessarily have been made by yet another missile.

Huey's corpse was viewed by a coroner's jury at the Rabenhorst Funeral Home, where it was being prepared to be laid out in state in the capitol's memorial hall for two days before the funeral. Thomas M. Davis, now a laboratory supervisor for an oil refinery, was one member of that five-man panel.

Speaking in the living room of his modest home in the Good-
wood subdivision, he recalls that——

"I was an L.S.U. freshman at the time. My daddy had
come to Baton Rouge from Alabama to work as a brickmason
at the Standard Oil plant. Dr. Tom Bird, the coroner, was a
friend of ours, and knew I wasn't too well fixed, so for as long
as I was in college, he would appoint me to these coroner's
juries because he knew the two-dollar fee I got helped me to
stay in school.

"The day of the inquest—it was a Tuesday and raining like
everything—we met at Rabenhorst's and were taken out in
back where Long's body lay under a sheet. The sheet was
lifted and then Dr. Tom, he raised up the right side of the
body to show us the wound in the back. It was so small I
doubt we'd have even seen it had it not been pointed out to
us. But they wouldn't let us get too close to the body, no
more than from here to the other side of the room [indicating
a distance of approximately twelve feet]. They never did let us
feel around to see could we get out another bullet. They did
show us the little old Spanish [sic!] automatic that belonged
to Dr. Weiss, and then Dr. Tom filled out the report and we
all signed it, and went home through the rain that was still
pouring. That afternoon Dr. Weiss was buried."

Long was buried two days later. Throughout the day and
night, Tuesday and Wednesday, his body lay in state as thousands upon thousands filed slowly past the casket in an apparently endless procession to look their last upon him. From
near and far came floral offerings: elaborate professional set
pieces of broken columns, gates ajar, open schoolbooks, and
the like, with ornately gold-lettered, broad ribbons of white
or lavender silk; but there were likewise many simple wreaths
of garden blossoms, plucked by the hands of those who re-
vered ol' Huey as the avatar who had been put on earth to
brighten and better the lot of the common man. Large as it

was, Memorial Hall could not begin to hold the flowers. When they were set up outdoors in the landscaped capitol park, they occupied literally acres of the grounds.

Beginning with daybreak on Thursday, mourners began to stream into Baton Rouge from all sections of the state; by special train from the cities, by chartered bus, by glossy limousine and mud-spattered farm pickup. Looking westward from the observation gallery atop the capitol's thirty-one-story central section, it is possible to see for nearly seven miles along one of the state's principal highways. No bridge had yet been built to span the Mississippi at this point. Consequently, as far as the eye could see from this lofty lookout platform, a solid line of vehicles was stalled. They moved forward only a bit at a time, as the Port Allen ferries, doing double duty, picked up deckload after deckload for transfer to the east bank.

Mrs. Long had asked Seymour Weiss to make all funeral arrangements, and because Huey, though nominally a Baptist, was not a church member and thought little of ministers as a class, the problem of selecting an ordained churchman to conduct the services was a sticky one. Religious prejudice was no part of Long's make-up. He had known Dick Leche as a close friend for years. Yet on the last day, when casting about for a gubernatorial candidate, he did not even know whether this close friend was or was not a Catholic.

Looking back on what happened, and still chagrined by the memory of his decision to select Gerald Smith as funeral chaplain, Seymour Weiss relates that "I didn't know what to do. If I picked a Catholic priest, a Protestant minister, or a rabbi, I'd offend those that weren't represented; even if I picked all three for a sort of joint service, those who felt that Huey was neither a Catholic nor a Jew might resent their inclusion, and in addition, the funeral service would be dragged out too long with three obituary sermons to deliver.

THE AFTERMATH   135

Then I happened to recall that Gerald Smith had severed his connection with a Shreveport church of which he had been the pastor before being employed by the Share-Our-Wealth movement as an exhorter.

"So I went to him and said: 'You're a kind of free-lance preacher without portfolio, and that's why I'm going to give you the biggest honor you've ever had. You're going to conduct Huey's funeral service' . . . and that was the worst mistake I ever made in all my life."

Not that anything untoward occurred to mar the service. Under direction of highway-department engineers, special crews had labored around the clock to have the vault ready. From the great bronze doors of the capitol the cortege was led by Castro Carrazo and his Louisiana State University student band. With drums muffled and the tempo of their march reduced to slow-step they played "Every Man a King," so artfully transposed to a minor key that what was and still is essentially a doggerel became an impressive and moving dirge. The service that followed was simple and dignified.

In Baltimore, Henry L. Mencken, ever ready to sacrifice fact for the turn of a sparkling phrase, predicted that ere long Louisianians would dynamite Huey's ornate casket out of its crypt and erect an equestrian statue of Dr. Weiss over the site. The truth is that a monument to the fallen apostle of Share-Our-Wealth has been built above the vault, and that elders still make worshipful pilgrimages to the spot.

Indeed, there have been those who literally canonized the memory of the man who once proclaimed himself Kingfish. Among the personal advertisements in the daily newspapers of South Louisiana one finds cards of thanks to this or to that favorite saint. "Thanks to St. Rita and St. Jude for financial aid." "Thanks to St. Anthony for successful journey." "Thanks to St. Joseph for recovery of father and husband." And among them have appeared such cards as this: "Thanks to

St. Raymond, St. Anthony, Sen. Huey P. Long for favor
granted." The last one cited appeared in the New Orleans
Times-Picayune of June 11, 1937.

Even those who make up a younger generation to whom
Huey Long's name already has become as impersonal as that
of, let us say, Millard Fillmore, still visit the statue, much as
they would pause to look at any other historical monument
in their travels.

Within twenty-four hours of the most elaborate funeral
ever held in Louisiana, attended by approximately 150,000
participants in the solemn rites of lamentation, Huey's
Praetorian Guard were up in arms against one another. Ready
to yield instant obedience to their Kingfish, they were one
and all determined never to render such homage to anyone of
their own subordinate rank.

The climax came about three o'clock one morning, when
Gerald Smith not only proclaimed himself the new head of
the Share-Our-Wealth movement, but announced the ticket
which he and his followers had endorsed and would back in
the forthcoming January primary. None of the names Huey
had been considering appeared thereon. It was headed by the
names of State Senator Noe for governor and Public Service
Commissioner Wade O. Martin, Sr., for United States senator.

Reverend Smith issued his pronouncement from the Roosevelt Hotel, but was incautious enough to tell such people
as Ray Daniell of the New York Times, Allen Raymond of
the New York Herald Tribune, and myself that the Huey
Long organization would move forward with even greater
strides as soon as it had rid itself of the Jews in it.

The reaction was so immediate it must have shocked even
him. The first obstacle he encountered was the announce-
ment by Earle Christenberry that no one not specifically
authorized to do so by himself as copyright owner, could use

either Share-Our-Wealth or Share-the-Wealth as party des-
ignations, and that he proposed to turn over the only membership rolls of that organization to Mrs. Long.

The next came when the other Long bigwigs, realizing
the ominous implications of Smith's bid for the scepter, sub-
merged all their intramural antagonisms in order to prevail
on Judge Leche, as the candidate the late Kingfish himself had
tapped, to head an "official" Long organization ticket. By
way of making this ticket's status all the more authentic, it
also carried the names of Earl Long as candidate for lieutenant governor, Oscar Allen as nominee to serve out Huey's
unexpired term in the Senate, and Allen Ellender as candidate
for the ensuing full six-year term, for which Huey himself
would have run as curtain raiser to his bid for the presidency.

In addition, Russell Long, then only seventeen years old,
was enlisted as one of the speakers who would campaign on
behalf of the official ticket. This was to be his initial bid for
political recognition; he was put on the first team, campaigning right alongside his uncle and Judge Leche. Gerald Smith,
on the other hand, was relegated to obviously subordinate
rank. Realizing the hopelessness of a maverick's lone foray
against such odds, to say nothing of his inability to secure
funds from the Share-Our-Wealth organization, he returned
to the fold, and was assigned to address rural meetings in
small country churches and the like.

By and large the platform of the authorized Long ticket
was simple: from the stump and in circulars, over the radio
and in newspaper advertising, the anti-Long slate was branded
the "Assassination Ticket."

Its backers were additionally handicapped by having Congressman Cleveland Dear, an Alexandria attorney and a very
inept campaigner, as their candidate. His insistence that he
headed a "Home Rule Ticket" which proposed to return to
individual communities those rights of self-government which

dictatorship had usurped, fell upon deaf ears. Even had Dear and his fellows been skilled and adroit campaigners, their prowess would have availed little against the hysterical determination of the great mass of voters to express by their ballots how deeply they disapproved of assassination—especially of the assassination of their idolized ol' Huey.

There was actually a pathetic overtone to Cleveland Dear's declaration that the hotel conference "was attended by about 300 of as fine men as can be found, who registered openly at the hotel desk, conducted their conversations openly in rooms and in hallways and not behind locked doors. There was hardly a meeting at that time where the possibility of bloodshed was not mentioned, but I heard no discussion of it at that hotel conference.

"Yet the governor is going around this state preaching hatred, and charging that the murder plot was hatched there. If he believes that, he should have me arrested. I challenge him to have me arrested!"

This sort of defensive jeremiad fell very flat when in country-school assembly halls, in churches, in fraternal-lodge rooms and other small rural meeting places, administration speakers became emotional over basins of red dye, lifting the fluid in cupped hands and letting it trickle back in the lamplight while declaiming: "Here it is, like the blood Huey Long shed for you, the blood that stained the floor as it poured from his body. Are you going to vote for those who planned this deed and carried it into execution?"

It soon became obvious to even the most optimistic leaders of the self-styled Home Rule faction that something must be done to stem the "assassination" tide. The climax was reached when Mayor Walmsley was booed to the echo by the throng that had come to see the first bridge ever built across the Mississippi at New Orleans formally dedicated and opened to traffic. The official name of the structure, and so marked

on War Department maps: the Huey P. Long Bridge. The
chorus of boos drowned out every word that Mayor Walmsley
uttered at the dedication, and was maintained until he resumed his seat.

Whether or not this incident precipitated the final effort
of the Home Rulers to escape the assassination onus in that
cheerless campaign no one can say at this late date. But a
charge by Dear in his next address before a large meeting gave
birth to the bodyguard-bullet story, or at least brought about
its acceptance as factual in many circles to this day.

"Isn't it true that one of Huey Long's bodyguards is in
a mental institution this very minute?" he cried dramatically.
"Is he not muttering to himself over and over again: 'I've
killed my best friend! I've killed my best friend! I've killed
my best friend!'?"

This was not true. Dear did not name the bodyguard supposedly thus afflicted, and the newspapers thought so little
of his outburst, or were so reluctant to risk a libel suit, that
they did not even include the quotation in their accounts of
the rally. But for some reason which now escapes the memory
of those who recall the incident, it was taken for granted that
the candidate had referred to Joe Messina.

Marching steadily toward a landslide victory by a larger
majority than had ever been cast for any other Louisiana
candidate for governor—even for the Kingfish himself—Judge
Leche was asked whether he knew anything about the basis,
if any, of the Dear statement; specifically, whether Joe Messina
was then or had been confined recently to a mental institution.

"I'd say yes to that," he replied. "At least, he is one of the
doorkeepers at the executive mansion, and whenever I think
of how crazy I am to give up a quiet, peaceful, dignified place
on the appeals bench for a chance to live in that mansion
four long years, I'd definitely class it as a madhouse."

None the less, the charge—a countercharge, really—that the bullet which ended Huey Long's life came from the gun of one of his bodyguards was repeated so often thereafter, and with so many elaborations, that it was permanently embedded in the twentieth-century folklore of Louisiana.

The Long machine, for the moment an invincible political juggernaut, rolled on to total victory; but without Huey's genius for organization, for expelling undesirables and recruiting replacements, and above all for having his absolute authority accepted by those serving under him, it ground to a halt and collapsed within three years.

Beyond doubt another factor in the swiftness with which a monolithic organization of incipiently national scope crumbled into nothingness was the realization that its treasury had disappeared. Naturally, every effort was made to trace this hoard of dollars and documents. In November of 1936, while the Long estate was still under probate, the safety-deposit box which the Riggs National Bank at Washington still held in the late Senator's name was opened in the presence of Mrs. Long, the deputy Register of Wills, Earle Christenberry, a bank official, and a representative of the Internal Revenue Service. It was found empty, stripped of the trove which Long told Seymour Weiss he had removed to another and secret place of concealment.

With no clue to the new depository to which the contents of this vault had been transferred, the search for it was as prolonged as it was bootless. Every key on the ring turned over to Mrs. Long by the Lady of the Lake Sanitarium after her husband's demise was examined. Only one of them proved to have any possible relation to safety-deposit boxes. On August 11, 1936, Earle Christenberry made a tracing or rubbing of this key, and sent it to the Yale and Towne Company at Stamford, Connecticut.

Four days later W. W. Herrgen of that firm replied: "The

key which you sent to me . . . is for one of our No. 3401-C safety deposit locks, and a search of our files shows that this key could be for use in a lock at the Whitney National Bank of New Orleans."

The Whitney, largest and most independent bank in New Orleans at the time, was for that very reason the last one Huey Long would have been likely to select. In any case, its officials reported that the key in question was not for any of the boxes in their vault. Of the money, aggregating what may well have been several million dollars—enough to finance an entire presidential campaign on the lavish scale to which Huey Long was accustomed—no trace has ever been found.

Even the sale of *My First Days in the White House* was pitifully small compared to what it would have been had its author lived to issue it as a campaign document.

Up to this day no one has been able to hazard a guess as to what was done with this accumulation of currency. Long had always levied a political tribute of two per cent on the salaries of all state employees. No effort was made to conceal this. Indeed, the Kingfish boasted that his support came from the people in small, regular individual contributions, and not in huge individual gifts from the swollen corporations, the money barons, and something called "the interests."

From 1919 to 1946 Elmer L. Irey was chief of the Treasury Department's Intelligence and Enforcement Division. Among other and perhaps lesser achievements, he had directed the investigation that finally landed Al Capone behind bars for income-tax evasion. In a 1948 book by Irey, "as told to William J. Slocum," one chapter deals with the Roosevelt administration's efforts to secure a thorough investigation of the income-tax returns filed (or not filed) by Huey Long, his top aides, and even some of their subordinates.

"We decided that the technique that had put Al Capone and his gang in jail would be reasonably applicable to Huey

Long and his gang," the Irey book avers in telling of the
investigation that Treasury Secretary Morgenthau ordered
within three days after he took office.

Evidence was gathered against the smaller fry first, and with
former Governor Dan Moody of Texas as counsel for the
Treasury Department, one of these lesser lights was con-
victed and sentenced to Atlanta in April 1935.

By autumn more evidence had been gathered against Long
himself. According to Irey's memoir, it "convinced Moody.
'I will go before the grand jury when it meets next month
and ask for an indictment against Long,' Moody told us.
. . . That conversation was held on September 7."

This was the very day on which, in the course of a round
of golf, Huey Long confided to Seymour Weiss not only that
enough cash and other campaign material was in hand to
finance his presidential race, but that all this accumulation
had been removed from the safety-deposit box he—Long—
had rented under his own name in the Riggs National Bank
in Washington.

It must not be forgotten that Long too had a highly pro-
ficient intelligence service, and that therefore he was beyond
question well aware that the T-men were busily seeking evidence to be used against him. He knew who their operatives
in Louisiana were, where their headquarters office in the
Masonic Temple Building was, and in general, exactly how
the Irey unit functioned. He had no illusions about their
knowledge of his Riggs Bank safety-deposit box. He knew how
they had traced such depositories in other cases, and also
that, in the past, variations of "this money does not belong to
me, it is merely the political campaign (etc., etc.) fund of our
association" had proved to be no valid defense.

Whether or not that is why he stripped the Riggs Bank
box of its contents no one can say. But it is certain that if
Long had lived, and Dan Moody had impounded the con-

tents of this box for evidence of unreported income, he would
have made a water haul. . . . The T-men brought to trial
only one other of the indictments pending against Long bigwigs; they considered it their strongest case, but the jurors
found the defendant "not guilty." It was not until the government filed charges of using the mails to defraud that convictions were obtained some three or four years later.

What it all came down to is this: the apparently impregna-
ble political structure created by Huey Long, and the hard-
and-fast line of cleavage that separated Long from anti-Long
while the Kingfish was present to maintain his dictatorial
hold on all phases of his organization, began to disintegrate
at 4:06 A.M. of September 10, 1935. As is almost invariably the
case, the dictatorship died with the dictator. After the Leche
landslide majority of 1936 the governor-designate epitomized
the result rather ruefully by observing:

"They didn't vote for or against a live governor; only for or
against a dead senator."

Today the Long faction, what there is of it, is just another
loosely knit political coalition. The number of those who still
recall the self-anointed Kingfish of the Lodge becomes smaller
with each passing day. . . . In the spring of 1962 Johnny
Carson, then a television quizmaster, asked a couple of contestants on his "Who Do You Trust?" program this question:

"What statesman who was elected governor in 1928, was
assassinated at Baton Rouge in 1935?"

The two contestants, who had otherwise proved themselves
reasonably well informed, simply looked blank. Neither of
them could give the answer.

Before many more years have gone by, Huey Pierce Long
will be just another vague figure out of a history text, and
there will no longer be any disputes about the architect of
his assassination, the manner in which it was carried out, or
the motives that prompted it. But in the meantime——

> *"One cool judgment is worth*
> *a thousand hasty counsels."*
>
> ———WOODROW WILSON

The various versions of "what really happened" during the assassination of Huey Long can be grouped into four general classes under some such headings as the following:

Dr. Weiss, unarmed, entered the capitol and merely struck at Long, being gunned down at once by the bodyguards, one of whose wild shots inflicted a mortal wound on the man they were seeking to defend.

Dr. Weiss was armed, did fire one shot which missed its target. In the ensuing fusillade which riddled the young physician's body, a wild shot inflicted on Long a wound which proved fatal.

The small-caliber bullet from Weiss's weapon did not pass completely through its victim's body, and was never found, being buried with him. The fatal bullet, a ricochet or stray shot from the gun of a bodyguard, was the missile that emerged from Long's body in the back, creasing the kidney in its passage and initiating what later proved to be a fatal hemorrhage.

Dr. Weiss's small-caliber weapon fired the only shot which struck Huey Long, passing through the right side of the abdomen, and injuring the right kidney just before emerging at the back. It is possible that surgery to remove this kidney, rather than the frontal laparotomy which was performed, might have halted the fatal hemorrhage and thus have saved Long's life.

Taking these up individually and in sequence, it becomes a relatively simple matter to dispose of the first assumption. This rests on the undeniable fact that Senator Long's lower lip bore an abrasion on its outer surface, and a small cut inside of his mouth; also on the statement of one nurse who is quoted as saying she heard the patient say in the hospital: "He hit me."

But there is abundant evidence to support the belief that if this bruise was the result of a blow, it was not struck by Dr. Weiss. There is, for one thing, the testimony of Sheriff Coleman, that he struck at Senator Long's assailant twice, that the first blow missed the assassin and struck someone else, and that the second felled Weiss, who by that time was grappling with Murphy Roden.

There is likewise the statement of the first physician to examine the gravely wounded man at the hospital, when Judge O'Connor voiced the belief that Long had been shot in the mouth because of the bloody spittle that stained his clothing. After an examination the young doctor declared "that is just where he hit himself against something."

There is the unanimous testimony of Justice Fournet, Sheriff Coleman, and Murphy Roden that the assailant later identified as Dr. Weiss did have "a small black pistol" and did fire it, as well as the testimony of Frampton, Justice Fournet, and Coleman that this pistol was lying a few inches from Dr. Weiss's lifeless hand immediately after the shooting.

But above all, the belief that the young physician was unarmed and merely struck Long with his fist is proved fallacious by one circumstance: the identity of the bullet-riddled body on the floor of the corridor where the shooting took place was not established until long after the weapon was found, in fact, not until the coroner arrived and examined the contents of the dead man's wallet.

It goes without saying that if Dr. Weiss came unarmed to the capitol, some other person must have brought his gun there from the car where his father testified he carried it. The argument is advanced that this was done by a bodyguard, a highway patrolman, or an officer of the state bureau of identification, to direct suspicion away from the "fact" that a wild shot from one of the bodyguards was the only missile that inflicted a mortal wound on Long.

But this presupposes that those who could not identify a riddled body on the marble floor of a capitol corridor were none the less able to pick out the slain man's automobile from among the hundreds, possibly thousands, of cars parked on the capitol grounds and along every nearby street, search it for a weapon, and place that weapon surreptitiously where it was picked up by the authorities moments after the shooting. This so far transcends even the most remote possibility, that any version based on the assumption that Weiss, unarmed, merely struck at Long with his fist, can be discarded out of hand.

The second category includes all versions of the proposition that Carl Weiss did fire one shot, but missed. There is even one account which holds that, at the time, Long was wearing a bullet-proof vest which Weiss's small-caliber bullet could not penetrate.

Everyone who knew Huey Long well, who traveled with him on his campaign tours, stopped at the same hotels with him, and so on, can testify to the fact that he was never known to wear a bullet-proof vest. He surrounded himself with armed guards wherever he went; a cadre of militiamen in full uniform, with steel helmets and side arms, accompanied him to the washroom in what is now the building of the National Bank of Commerce while he was conducting one of his murder-plot probes there. But he wore no armor.

Of my own knowledge I can testify that I have seen him in his suites at the Roosevelt and at the Heidelberg when, after breakfast, he bathed and dressed for the street, that I have traveled with him during his campaigns through Louisiana and through Arkansas, that I have been with him in his home on Audubon Boulevard, and that never, from the day I first met him in 1919 to the day of his death in 1935, have I known him to wear anything that remotely resembled a bullet-proof vest.

But to make assurance doubly sure, I checked this point with Earle Christenberry and with Seymour Weiss, his two closest friends.

"I can't imagine how that story got about," Christenberry said, "but I know exactly on what it must be based. About six months before Huey died I got the bright idea that it would be a smart thing for him, when he went out stumping the country in the approaching presidential campaign, to wear a bullet-proof vest. So without saying a word to him about it, I wrote to Elliott Wisbrod in Chicago, a manufacturer of such equipment, and asked that a vest of this type be sent to me for the Senator's approval.

"The thing was delivered in due course, and I put it on and went to his room and showed it to him, and suggested that on occasion it might be wise to wear it as a protection against some unpredictable attack. He told me to send the damn thing back, adding 'it would be ridiculous for me to wear it. I don't need no goddam bullet-proof vest.' So I sent it back and that was the end of it.

"I have never spoken about this incident from that day to this. I didn't think another soul knew about it. But evidently the story must have leaked out somewhere; from the manufacturers, I suppose. At any rate, I was the one that wore the bullet-proof vest, one day for a few minutes. He never did in all his life."

Seymour Weiss, the sartorial mentor who weaned Long away from the flashy clothes in which he first came to public notice, put it more succinctly.

"Huey wouldn't have known what a bullet-proof vest looked like," he said.

Other aspects of the available evidence cover not merely the category of stories about Weiss's bullet missing its target, being deflected by a bullet-proof vest, etc., but the next category as well. This embraces what is far and away the most widely believed and oft repeated version of what took place. It holds that a bullet from the gun of a bodyguard inflicted the mortal wound of whose effects Huey Long died, even though Dr. Weiss's small-caliber missile likewise struck him.

Three points are the ones most frequently stressed by those who cling to this theory.

The first is that "no small-caliber bullet was ever found." This has been interpreted to mean that the Weiss bullet was still in Long's body and, no autopsy being authorized, was buried with him. There is general agreement on one point. The fatal injury was sustained near the wound of exit, in the region of the right kidney. It was there that a continuing hemorrhage was the immediate cause of death.

The argument runs that Weiss's bullet of small caliber never having been found, and therefore remaining in the body of the victim, the wound of exit must have been made by some other bullet. No other bullet was fired by anyone except the bodyguards, who discharged a wild barrage of pistol fire which left the body of Dr. Weiss riddled with wounds, and pocked the marble walls of the corridor with bullet scars which for years official guides pointed out to visitors touring the capitol. The injury near the point of exit was the only demonstrably fatal one; ergo, a bodyguard's bullet killed Long.

The view that the Kingfish perished from the effects of a bullet-wound inflicted by one of his own guards also had a certain superficial plausibility that appealed strongly to dedicated leaders of anti-Long factionalism and their followers. It carried with it an overtone of Matthew's "All-they-that-take-the-sword-shall-perish-with-the-sword" retributive justice. Finally it was labored in season and out by the Home Rule campaign speakers who sought to rid themselves of the Assassination Ticket stigma by proving that Long had died at the hands of one of his own men.

It would be difficult to overestimate the fashion in which all this tended to perpetuate what began as a campaign legend. For example, Elmer Irey, whose career as postal inspector and finally chief of the Treasury Department's Intelligence Division spanned more than a generation, assuredly must be accounted a professional in the realm of gathering, sifting, and assaying evidence. Yet in his book he reports that——

"Weiss had a .22 calibre pistol in his hand when Long's bodyguards mowed him down. Long died as the result of a single bullet wound made by a .45 calibre slug. Nobody has explained that yet."

To cite still another instance, I happened to meet both Isaac Don Levine (author of, among other works, *The Mind of an Assassin*) and Dr. Alton Ochsner at a medical gathering some years ago, not long after Dr. Vidrine's death. The talk turned on the events of the night when Huey Long died.

"Why, I always thought it was a bodyguard, not Dr. Weiss, who killed Long!" exclaimed Levine. When I spoke of some of the contradictions to which this view was open, Dr. Ochsner expressed amazed disbelief that any presumably informed person could entertain the slightest doubt that Long's death was due to a bodyguard's bullet or bullets.

And yet the weight of all real evidence is wholly against

this hypothesis; so much so, in fact, that it is difficult to select a point of approach to it. For a beginning, then, one must take into account the "small, blue punctures" a bullet left on Huey Long's body as the mark of its passage. Only one photograph of Dr. Weiss's body was ever taken. The official photographer of the State Bureau of Identification made this picture, which has never before been published. It shows the great gaping wounds left on his torso by the .44- and .45-caliber bullets of those who fired into his already lifeless body. Most of the large-caliber cartridges also carried hollow-point bullets, which have a mushrooming effect. (Cf. Murphy Roden's "I saw the flesh open up," when he fired into Weiss's throat as they were locked in a fierce struggle on the corridor floor.)

Granted that a wildly ricocheting bullet from one of these guns could have entered into the same wound made by Dr. Weiss's small-caliber bullet, unlikely as this may seem, it could by no stretch of the long arm of coincidence have made its exit as a small bluish puncture. Even if it alone caused the wound of exit, leaving a small bullet still in the body of its victim, the point at which it plowed its way out of Long's back would have been a gaping orifice and not, as Thomas Davis graphically described it, "so small I doubt we'd have seen it had it not been pointed out to us."

Another fact not to be overlooked is that the moment Dr. Rives saw the clean dressing that had been placed over the wound and the operational incision in the anterior wall of Long's abdomen, he came to the conclusion that any bullet entering at that point in the manner described, most probably emerged in the area of the kidney, and was likely to have damaged that organ. It was for this reason that he asked whether any blood had been found in the patient's urine, learning to his astonishment that the critically wounded man

had not even been catheterized to determine the existence
and extent of kidney damage.

The visible abdominal trauma disclosed by the Vidrine
operation was small; so small that only a small-caliber bullet
could have caused it. Two holes had been left in the large
bowel at the bend where it turns horizontally across the abdomen from right to left. These holes were so small that there
was "very little soilage." Reports that when the abdomen
was opened by Vidrine it was "a mass of blood and fecal
matter" were simply fabrications into which a minute fragment of fact was expanded, like some of Huey Long's murder-plot charges.

Finally, the available evidence is conclusive in one respect:
By the time the bodyguard fusillade began, Huey Long had
fled the corridor where the shooting took place. Coleman,
Frampton, and Fournet are unanimous on that point. Roden,
blinded by the searing muzzle blasts of his comrades' guns,
could no longer see what was going on, but testifies that the
other guards waited until he had struggled to his knees from
beneath the lifeless body of Carl Weiss, before they started
their volley. O'Connor describes how the firing was still audible after Huey had reeled down four short flights of steps and
was being led out of a ground-floor door into the porte-
cochere.

In sum, every item of credible evidence—surgical, circumstantial, and the testimony of eyewitnesses—indicates that
Huey Long could not have been struck by a bullet from the
gun of one of his bodyguards. That leaves but one other
conceivable hypothesis, namely: Huey Long died of the effects of a bullet wound inflicted by Carl Weiss and no one
else.

Disregarding the physical circumstances, an intangible consideration virtually compels the acceptance of this view. We
have in the testimony of all the eyewitnesses a substantial

agreement on what took place. Roden, Fournet, and Coleman saw the gun in Weiss's hand and saw him fire it. Frampton, Coleman, and Fournet saw and describe Long's flight before the crashing salvo by the other bodyguards began.

Their stories differ in detail. Frampton says Huey gave "a sort of a grunt" when he was shot; Justice Fournet describes it as "a hoot." He also says the first shot was fired by Weiss, the next three by Coleman; Roden says the first two shots were fired by Weiss, the third by himself, and the fourth by someone else (obviously Coleman). Coleman says Huey was attended by Roden, McQuiston, and himself on his final visit to the House chamber, Fournet says he was accompanied by Messina, and Frampton reports that Messina answered the telephone in the office of the sergeant at arms, which opens off the Speaker's rostrum and is entirely separate from the House chamber.

These discrepancies are natural; only the absence of such variations would lay the testimony of witnesses to a violent incident open to the suspicion, nay the certainty, of collusion. Take for example the three mutually contradictory versions of what happened when the two principals, Roden and Weiss, locked in literally a life-and-death grapple, fell struggling to the floor. Roden says his hard heels slipped on the marble paving; Justice Fournet says he threw out his hands in a gesture that overbalanced the two; Coleman says a blow of his fist felled Weiss, who, clasped in Roden's grip, pulled the latter down beneath him.

But on the main point—namely, that the two fell to the floor, and that Weiss was not killed until after they were down—all are in complete agreement. If it is assumed that this is a concocted story, made up to divert suspicion from one or more of the bodyguards as having fired so wildly that one of their bullets brought about their leader's death, the following must likewise be accepted as true:

Somewhere and sometime before the first of these four witnesses told what he saw, all of them would have had to agree on the specific untruths they would tell.

But at no time was there any opportunity during those initial frantic moments for the four to have met, either to concoct and agree on a false story or for any other purpose. Indeed, Frampton was already telephoning his first story of what had occurred, while the others are all accounted for elsewhere: Coleman describing to Governor Allen what he had seen, Justice Fournet in the hospital, Roden out of action and temporarily blinded until taken to the hospital himself by Ty Campbell.

Furthermore, after treatment, and not having spoken to any others in the meantime, Roden gave his statement that night to General Guerre, and later to General Fleming. These accounts agreed in almost every detail with one another and with the one he gave me, twenty-four years later, in the presence of Generals Fleming and Guerre, who verified that this statement differed in no essential respect from what he had told them at the scene when questioned by them on the night of September 8, 1935.

Except for one detail, it also agrees with the testimony he gave on September 16 of that same year, at the Odom inquest. It was his belief at first that Dr. Weiss fired but once. However, mulling the violent images of that night over in his mind, he later came to the conclusion that the doctor fired twice; this, incidentally, is the only conclusion that would square with the two minor injuries he sustained on his right hand and left wrist.

In any case, the possibility of conspiratorial collusion among these four in time to have agreed on a falsified account of what took place before their eyes, would appear to be ruled out in its entirety. The inevitable corollary of such a proposition is that the otherwise uncontradicted testimony of these four witnesses is a factual account of what took place.

None the less, one cannot dismiss out of hand the possibility, however remote, that evidence can be framed, as it has been in documented cases—Sacco-Vanzetti, Tom Moony, Leo M. Frank; and that circumstantial evidence, even where no single link in the chain appears weak, leads now and then to false conclusions. But it can be said that in this instance the overwhelming weight of available evidence indicates that Weiss's bullet was the cause of Huey Long's death, and that no bullet from the guns of one or another of his bodyguards was a contributing factor in putting an end to his career.

The available evidence likewise appears to indicate beyond a reasonable doubt that the emergency operation was a contributing cause of death in the following respect:

Had a decision to perform a frontal laparotomy been deferred, and had in its stead a removal of the damaged right kidney made possible the tying off of the blood vessels supplying this organ to halt the hemorrhage that was draining off the victim's life blood, Huey Long might none the less have died of peritonitis, from "soilage" into the abdominal cavity by the two small punctures of the large bowel.

But once the decision to operate from the front was carried into effect, the only door to possible—by no means "certain," but possible—recovery was irrevocably closed. Even Dr. Vidrine realized that a second operation to halt the kidney hemorrhage was something his patient could not survive.

By way of conclusion it is logical to say that on the basis of available testimony and with due regard for the imminence of human error, the following facts appear to be established by the overwhelming preponderance of evidence:

Dr. Weiss was armed when he went into the capitol building on the night of September 8, 1935, carrying with him the small-caliber Belgian automatic he had brought back from

France and which he customarily took with him in his car on night calls.

According to the integrated testimony of four eyewitnesses who had no opportunity for collusion prior to giving their accounts of what they saw, he held the gun in one hand, concealing it with the straw hat he held in the other, so that it was virtually impossible for him to have struck a blow with his fist.

Every trustworthy piece of testimony appears to make it clear that only four shots were fired while Huey Long was on the scene: two by Weiss, one each by Roden and Coleman; that by the time the general bodyguard fusillade began, the Senator was already on his way down a flight of stairs opposite the Western Union office, which is around a corner from the site of the shooting; and that the fusillade was still in progress while Long was being led out of the building by Judge O'Connor.

Medical testimony is unanimous on the point that only one bullet, and that one of small caliber, traversed Long's abdomen, leaving small blue punctures at the points of entry and exit; that the primarily fatal injury was caused when, just prior to its exit, the bullet damaged the victim's right kidney at a point where only removal of the maimed organ could have halted the ensuing and ultimately fatal hemorrhage.

Granted then, if only for the sake of argument, that there no longer is either mystery or even reasonable doubt concerning *who* killed Huey Long, one big, crucial question remains unanswered. It is this:

"*Why?*"

> *"Life is the art of drawing suffi-*
> *cient conclusions from insuffi-*
> *cient premises."*
> ——SAMUEL BUTLER

The difficulty encountered when seeking to rationalize the assassination of Huey Long is implicit in two circumstances. The first is the total absence of fact or testimony about the motive for it, so that conclusions are necessarily based on surmise.

The second is the apparently irreconcilable disparity between the known nature of Carl Weiss, the man, and the obvious nature of his act. Why would someone whose closest personal and professional associates unhesitatingly declare him to have been incapable of any dark deed of violence commit a murder by shooting down an unsuspecting victim as if from ambush? What could conceivably account for the metamorphosis of a mild, retiring young man, happily married and fulfilled in the birth of a dearly beloved son, into an indomitably resolute killer, ready to sacrifice his own life, rich with promise, in order to take the life of another?

In this instance the problem is not merely one of drawing sufficient conclusions from insufficient premises. Conclusions must be drawn from *two* mutually contradictory sets of insufficient premises.

Barry O'Meara, the Irish ship's surgeon aboard the vessel that brought Napoleon to St. Helena, volunteered to remain

there with him, but was one of the first to be deported when
Sir Hudson Lowe subsequently took over the governorship of
the island. He was one of the fallen emperor's few confidants
during the desolate days of that terminal exile. In his memoirs
of their association he quoted Napoleon as saying:

"A man is known by his conduct to his wife, to his family,
and to those under him."

The members of Carl Weiss's family are still not convinced,
or at least are still unwilling to admit, that he took Long's
life. The nurses who were his principal subordinates, and
many of whom still survive, looked on him not merely as a
physician, but as a teacher. To this day they agree he could
not have done what all available evidence conclusively proves
that he did.

Miss Theoda Carriere, the first registered nurse called to
attend Senator Long after the shooting, now lives in a piny
woods retreat near Amite. "Dr. Weiss just wasn't the kind of
person who would do a thing like that," she insists. "He
taught us chemistry when we were in training, and every girl
in our class looked on him as one of the gentlest and kindest
of men. None of us believe he was the one who shot Long."

Admittedly, Dr. Chester A. Williams, Jr., the present coroner of East Baton Rouge parish, cannot be regarded as a
Long partisan. It was he who pronounced Earl Long insane in
1959 while the latter was still governor, and committed him
to a mental institution. Yet he set down the following re-
strained obiter dictum after transcribing and studying the
microfilmed hospital chart of Huey Long's final hours:

"Most of the doctors who lived in Baton Rouge and are
still living do not feel that Dr. Weiss shot Long."

In a strictly technical sense, only Carl Weiss himself, his
lips irrevocably sealed within seconds after he did what "his
family and those under him," not to mention his professional

associates, still regard him as incapable of doing, could have given a conclusive solution to this paradox.

Since that is out of the question, the best that can now be done is to list the various possible motives which either have been or could be considered as impelling Dr. Weiss to sacrifice his own life in order to put an end to that of Huey Long. From the roster thus compiled, the obviously impossible and then the logically infirm assumptions can be eliminated one by one, to see whether any hypothesis which might fit such of the facts as are ascertainable will withstand searching scrutiny.

Four motives have been or can be imputed to Dr. Weiss in connection with the shooting of Long. They are:

The young physician was the executioner chosen by a group of plotters in a cabal of which he was a member, to carry out the death sentence there secretly decreed against an otherwise invincible political oppressor.

The assassination was an act of reprisal for the gerrymander which would bring to an abrupt end the twenty-eight-year judicial career of Yvonne Weiss's father through a fraudulent mockery of legislative procedure deliberately rigged to deny the parish of St. Landry the free exercise of home rule.

An abstract idealism inspired a quixotic young patriot to sacrifice himself on the altar of the common weal by destroying a dictatorship through the death of the autocrat who stood at its head.

Haunted by anxiety born of a suspicion that, in campaigning against Judge Pavy, Long would raise the specter of an all-but-forgotten and long since refuted racial slur against the Pavy family, Dr. Weiss paid with his life for the assurance that libelous words resurrecting the false stigma would never be uttered.

The first of these four propositions can be given short shrift. The Senate speech in which Long sought to implicate the Roosevelt administration, and in effect President Roosevelt himself, in a "plan of robbery, murder, blackmail, or theft" was the latest of several revelations charging others with plotting his murder. It happened also to be the last one because within a month after making this charge in the Senate, he was assassinated.

But significant factors must not be overlooked. The first is that after none of these spectacular accusations of murder plots was anyone ever formally charged before any court with conspiracy to commit murder.

The second is the undeniable fact that the so-called murder conference in the De Soto Hotel was neither more nor less than a political caucus of the type customarily held behind closed doors in order to facilitate full freedom of discussion about personalities, political prospects, and the like.

The third is that when all the verbiage about patronage plums and job distribution and endorsement of candidacies is sifted for substance, a pitiably small modicum of grain is recovered from a mountain of chaff. Here are the only specific references to the infliction of bodily harm by those hotel conferees actually quoted by Long in his Senate speech:

Oscar Whilden is reported as saying: "I am out to murder, bulldoze, steal, or anything else to win this election." An unidentified voice said: "I would draw in a lottery to go out and kill Long. It would only take one man, one gun, one bullet." Another unidentified voice said: "I haven't the slightest doubt but that Roosevelt would pardon anyone who killed Long." And still another unidentified voice said: "The best way would be to just hang around Washington and kill him in the Senate."

These four remarks were sandwiched in among two days of political discussion about an approaching state campaign, the selection of candidates, the use of federal patronage, and matters of that sort! By way of illustration, a remark in a recent magazine article about another Louisiana representative, Congressman Otto Passman, would offer a much firmer foundation for a conspiracy charge along the lines followed by Long.

Passman has dedicated himself, in season and out, to opposing and reducing foreign-aid appropriations, and President Kennedy is quoted as asking at the signing ceremony of one of these bills: "What am I going to do about Passman?"

"Mr. President," a bystander is reported as replying, "you're surrounded by a lot of well-armed Secret Service Men. Why don't you have one of them shoot him—by accident, of course? In fact, Mr. President, if you promise me immunity, I'll do it myself."

No one who read that statement took it in its literal sense; no one regarded it as a serious proposal to authorize, commit, and condone the murder of a legislator. Yet that is precisely the construction Huey Long put on four similar remarks made at intervals during a two-day caucus in a New Orleans hotel.

All this would tend to cast doubts upon the complicity of Carl Weiss in a murder conspiracy, even had he been the sort of person to whom a deed involving assassination would normally have been possible. However, what removes the assumption that he was the chosen executioner of a political camarilla from serious consideration is this:

Carl Weiss was virtually unknown outside of his immediate professional, social, and familial circle. Not one of the leading supposed "plotters" of the hotel conference spoke of him during that meeting, none of the leaders who were asked about him later could recall having heard of him, although his wife's father and uncle were known to virtually all of them.

In sum, the hotel meeting of which Long sought to make

great capital was not a murder conference, and no one dreamed of bringing to book on charges of criminal conspiracy any of those who took part in it; and even had it been such a conspiracy, the name of Carl Weiss was not even remotely connected with it.

The second proposition would have it that Carl Weiss assassinated Long in reprisal for what the latter was doing to Yvonne's father by having him gerrymandered out of office, and virtually out of public life. There are those who go so far as to say that Yvonne goaded her young husband into exacting satisfaction from the despot who was persecuting her family, who had brought about the dismissal of her uncle Paul from a school superintendency, and of her sister Marie from a position as teacher, and who was now implacably going to any lengths to close her father's long and honorable career as judge.

The whole idea of such a reprisal motive runs directly counter to every fact known about the way the Weiss families passed that last Sunday: the young couple leaving the baby with their elders while they attended Mass, the family dinner at which the gerrymander was indeed the topic of conversation, but in a light, rather jocular vein; the young couple "sporting in the water" at the elders' camp in the afternoon, while the latter fondled their precious grandson, the domestic routine that preceded Carl's departure for a professional call. . . .

As nearly as anything human can be certain, it is sure that neither Dr. Weiss nor any of the Pavy clan would ever have dreamed of taking upon their consciences the killing of a fellow being, even in the heat of passion, over such a matter as the loss of a public office, a development they had discussed almost jocularly only a few hours before.

Only two theoretical assumptions thus remain as to the motive of Dr. Weiss in committing a violent act contrary to

all that was known of his nature. One is the idea advanced
by Yvonne's uncle, Dr. Pavy, that this was "an act of pure
patriotism." In 1935, when Dr. Pavy served as spokesman for
the Weiss family, he felt that his niece's husband was deeply
troubled by "the suppressive type of government" that had
been imposed on Louisiana; that he brooded over this until
"his mind unhinged," and he determined to put an end to
the dictatorship even at the cost of his life.

Supporting this view are certain plausible factors. Carl
Weiss was indeed an idealist of the type who might voluntarily
have sacrificed his life in the furtherance of any noble cause,
such as the liberation of his community from the thralldom
imposed upon it by a ruthless authoritarian. Negating this
view, however, is the fact that he took no active part in politics, though at that time Baton Rouge, his home, was the
focal point of fiercely contested Long and anti-Long rivalry.

It is simply not conceivable, in the general sense of that
word, that anyone so deeply and earnestly concerned with
"pure patriotism" should not have been known to a single
member of the press gallery at the capitol, to a single member
of the State Bureau of Identification, to so well known a
leader of the anti-Long movement in Baton Rouge as Dr.
Tom Bird—a fellow physician—and above all, to Huey Long
himself, a man whose memory for names and faces was truly
phenomenal.

While Carl Weiss could well have been a crusader for any
idealistic cause, it is difficult to accept unreservedly the proposition that one who had so very much to live for, whose hap-
piness was so nearly complete, the best and most rewarding
years of whose life still lay in the future, would give up all
this and burden his conscience with two mortal sins—murder
and what was tantamount to self-destruction—for an abstract
concept of the general good.

It would seem almost self-evident that no man would voluntarily make such a sacrifice except in seeking to protect from harm those whom he held dear.

And there must have been some such motive in the haunting suspicion that, while campaigning against Judge Pavy, Huey Long would revive that long-buried, long-refuted tar-brush bugaboo which had been brought up unsuccessfully as involving one of Judge Pavy's relatives-in-law thirty years before.

In view of Long's past obsession with racial issues of this sort, Carl Weiss had good grounds for apprehension on that score. In past campaigns and polemics Long had never hesitated to use such innuendos, as when he referred to a prominent Orleanian as "Kinky" Soandso in issue after issue of his weekly newspaper, *The American Progress*. Nor had he hesitated to make direct attacks on this front, as in his campaigns against Dudley LeBlanc in the matter of the latter's Negro fellow officers of his burial-insurance society.

In his fancy the young physician could readily imagine Long's insistence that "this isn't what I'm saying; I'm not even a-saying it's so. All I'm telling you is this is what Sheriff Swords said time after time. . . ."

If Long, true to form, had made up his mind to drag this rejected canard back into the open, there was one sure way in which Dr. Weiss could keep him from his purpose and prevent a single syllable of that baseless and forgotten slander from being uttered. True, he could accomplish this only at the cost of his life. Surrounded as the Kingfish was by heavily armed guards, anyone who attacked him, even though he cut him down with the first shot, was sure to die himself, in the next instant, under a rain of bullets. Carl Weiss "just wasn't the sort of person that would ever do a thing like that," for any ordinary motive. But to shield the wife he adored and the infant son he idolized from a slander, groundless though it be, that would impute to them by innuendo a remote trace of Negro blood, he could—and in the opinion of many he did—lay down his life.

In that case, the real tragedy inherent in his act was not the sacrifice of his own future, so rich with promise, nor even the extinction of Huey Long, one of the most notable, challenging, and controversial figures in the public life of his era. Unschooled in the labyrinthine windings and turnings of politics in general and more particularly the ins and outs of Louisiana's politics during that hectic era, Dr. Weiss had no intimation of the fact that nothing could have been farther from Huey Long's plans than raising any racial issue at this time.

He did not know that Long was preparing to challenge Franklin Roosevelt's bid for re-election by running against him for the presidency; that he was no longer campaigning merely in the Deep South where Negroes, disfranchised ever since the final rout of carpetbaggery in the 1870s, were kept from the polls first by force, then by the Grandfather Clause, and after that by the Understanding Clause, but above all by the one-party device of settling campaigns not at a general election but in a Democratic (i.e., white) primary.

Running for office as the nominee of what in all likelihood would have been a new coalition party—the Share-Our-Wealthers?—Louisiana's Kingfish would need all the minority-group votes he could attract to his standard. Primarily this meant the heavy Negro vote of Harlem in New York, Chicago's black-and-tan belt, and other such concentrations in Boston, Philadelphia, Cleveland, Detroit, Cincinnati, and so on.

Looking forward, planning far ahead, he had already begun to rid himself of the "racist" label customarily applied to every far-Southern politician. As an initial step he abolished the poll tax in Louisiana, issuing poll certificates free to all applicants, regardless of color, provided they could meet the age and residential requirements.

True, this was quite meaningless insofar as enfranchising the Louisiana Negroes went. The law provided that no one would be permitted to register or to vote unless he could show poll-tax receipts (or later, free poll certificates) for each of the two years directly preceding any given election. Its intent was primarily to keep floaters from being brought into the state from Mississippi or other adjacent areas, on election day. But this was by no means the only prerequisite for voting. One must also be registered, each parish registrar being the sole arbiter as to whether the applicant had correctly interpreted a section of the state or federal constitutions.

In theory the Democratic Party was a private organization, like the Fifth Ward Athletic Guild, and could thus choose its members at pleasure, excluding whom it wished not to admit. Coupled with this was an unwritten agreement to settle political differences not between parties, but between factions of the Democratic Party, with all hands pledged to support the Democratic nominee in the ensuing general election, even if that nominee "happens to be a yellow dog!"

Abolition of the poll tax did nothing to alter this situation, which obtained until the Supreme Court invalidated it, many years after Long's death. None the less, Negroes queued up by the thousands and treasured the essentially worthless but to them invaluable slips of paper officially issued to them.

The next step was Huey's Share-Our-Wealth promise that this movement would recognize no racial bars of any sort, that the division of shared wealth would include black as well as white on equal terms. "Five thousand a year and a span of mules," the poor and underprivileged of both races told one another ecstatically. "With what I'm making now and the five thousand Huey Long's going to give us, we'll be in high cotton for true!"

The final step would have been some sort of a second Emancipation Proclamation, issued as a campaign document to a mammoth 1936 Share-Our-Wealth convention to be held in Detroit, or possibly St. Louis. The unmistakable augury of this was Huey Long's published apology during the summer of 1935 for having used the word *nigger* in the course of a national network broadcast. A "race" tabloid, referring to the word he had used as "the epithet n——r," sent a reporter to him in his suite at the New Yorker Hotel, and published the ensuing interview under a two-column headline on its front page. In his statement Long made it plain his use of "the epithet n——r" was a slip of the tongue, and was not meant to be derogatory in a racial sense; also that he would exercise due care not to use the epithet again in either public or private speech.

It is all but impossible to convey to non-Southerners how radical a departure from the *mores* of Winn parish in central Louisiana was this sort of retraction. Efforts were made to use the interview as an anti-Long campaign document. Facsimiles of the front page of the Negro tabloid were printed by some of the rural weeklies, but it didn't work. The Negro Share-Our-Wealthers throughout the land rejoiced. The whites in the organization shrugged it aside as fabricated anti-Long propaganda inspired by "the interests" or passed it off with: "As long as I get my five thousand a year, what difference does it make who else gets it too?"

It should not be overlooked that in the case of Judge Pavy, Long needed no resort to ancient libels to accomplish his longtime opponent's defeat. The gerrymander would make it impossible for Ben Pavy to be re-elected. Long would take the stump against him, of course, in order to claim the foreordained victory as another personal triumph; but once St. Landry parish was put into the same judicial district with Acadia, Lafayette, and Vermillion parishes, even the slightest possibility of a Pavy election was precluded. Huey Long would no more have gone to needless lengths to win an already

certain victory at the risk of alienating any large section of
the prospective Negro presidential vote than he would have
belabored a dying horse at an S.P.C.A. picnic in an effort to
make the animal run.

Taking all the foregoing into account, it would seem clearly
impossible to accept either the hypothesis that Carl Weiss,
Jr., was the chosen instrument of a political murder cabal to
whose membership he was almost wholly unknown, or the
proposition that his was a nature sufficiently ruthless to take
the life of a fellow being in reprisal for the loss of a long-held
political office by his wife's father.

As concerns the idea that Dr. Weiss was motivated by the
"pure patriotism" ascribed to him by his wife's uncle, Dr.
Pavy, there can be little doubt that this was possible. But it
is also not to be doubted that there is a basis beyond parental
affection for the elder Dr. Weiss's statement at the inquest
into his son's death that "my son was too superbly happy with
his wife and child, too much in love with them to want to
end his life after such a murder."

On the other hand, no such contradiction is an integral
part of the hypothesis that he made this sacrifice to shield
his wife and his son from exposure to groundless odium. This
would appear to be the only assumption in full accord with
all the known circumstances, even though Dr. Weiss's belief that Huey Long would exhume a long-buried slander re-
flecting on his loved ones was tragically erroneous.

On the basis of the situation as he saw and understood it,
the only way to safeguard them was to silence Long before
he could utter the libel. If the only price at which this assurance could be purchased was the forfeit of his own life, the
compulsive paternal urge to protect his beloved baby son
might well be strong enough to overcome every inhibition
that was normally part of his character and background. He
took no one into his confidence, realizing that anyone to

whom he confided would inevitably thwart his plan. Thus we may picture him leaving to his family the happy memory of an afternoon of carefree affection, and departing alone to weigh in solitude one factor of the situation against another, as he understood them.

Should he thereupon have decided that "this man will never slander my son as he has slandered others in the past if I can silence him," we can only surmise that it was with this thought in mind that he entered the marble-walled corridor where he died to make certain that some words Huey Long never intended to utter would remain unsaid.

EPILOGUE

> *"Finality is not the language of politics."*
>
> ———DISRAELI

To the Huey Long murder case the preceding chapters offer a solution which fits every determinate fact of what took place in Baton Rouge on September 8, 1935, everything pertinent that led up to the climactic moment of violence, and what followed. Yet it goes without saying that many will reject this rationalization of available evidence. The arguments will go on and on.

We are prone to cherish certain myths. As though in wish-fulfillment we still tell our children Parson Weems's absurd fable of the boy Washington, the cherry tree, and "I did it with my little hatchet." Similarly, the myth of the body-guard's bullet, product of a compulsive necessity for political escape from the onus of assassination, will retain adherents and win fresh believers, despite the obvious fact that wherever else the truth may lie, the bodyguard-bullet hypothesis is false.

Paradox remains a continuing footnote to Huey Long's career. Surrounded by fanatically loyal bodyguards, he was none the less done to death by a shy, retiring young stranger in whom neither he nor his myrmidons recognized any trace of menace. His injuries were critical and might in any case have proved fatal; but it was a decision on the part of the same Arthur Vidrine whom Huey Long had elevated to high command which sealed the Kingfish's doom. True, the alternative Dr. Vidrine chose was one many another physician, confronted by the same circumstances, might have selected inasmuch as mere delay in taking action could have proved fatal.

On the other hand, it is not to be disputed that Dr. Vidrine's decision to operate by a frontal incision made it impossible for him or any one else thereafter to save Huey Long's life. In consequence, he fell under the ban of the Long faction's permanent and extreme displeasure. As soon as he took office in 1936, Governor Leche appointed Dr. George Bel to the superintendency of Charity Hospital, thus automatically displacing Vidrine from that position. Within the year, Dr. James Monroe Smith, president of the State University, speaking for its Board of Supervisors, notified him that Dr. Rigney D'Aunoy had been made acting dean of the medical school but that he—Dr. Vidrine—might retain a place on the faculty as professor of gynecology.

Rather than accept such a demotion he resigned in August of 1937. Returning to Ville Platte, he founded a private hospital there, and maintained it until his retirement in ill health from active practice in 1950. Five years later he died.

Death also thwarted Long's design to place the Pavy gerrymander at the head of what became his last demonstration of dictatorship as the legislature's Act Number One. It became Act Number Three, since the first two were concurrent resolutions, one expressing the grief of House and Senate over the leader's untimely end, the other creating a committee to select a burial place on the capitol grounds for what remained of his physical presence among them.

As for the gerrymander, it never really took effect, though it automatically became law twenty days after the legislature adjourned. To be sure, it did provide for an additional

judge in a newly enlarged judicial district, he to be chosen
some fourteen months later at the time of the Congressional
election of November 1936.

But a new legislature, meeting in May 1936, adopted another statute, superseding this law and reshuffling Louisiana's
judicial districts once more to add a new one—the twenty-
seventh—consisting of St. Landry parish alone. This act, a
constitutional amendment, would not become operative until ratified by popular vote at the November elections. That
obviously made it impossible to elect a judge at the same
time, so the new bill provided that within thirty days after
its ratification, the governor should *appoint* a judge for the
new district, his term not to end until that of the judges
elected in 1936 should have run its course. In other words,
the appointee would serve for six years.

Needless to say, the appointee was not Benjamin Pavy.

Another facet of the Long paradox is presented by the
saint-or-sinner image which his contemporaries and their suc-
cessors yet seek to preserve. Until the Kingfish's name has
lost all popular significance, debates will be waged over the
issue of whether the man was an uninhibited genius, or merely
a conscienceless opportunist endowed with exceptional mental agility. On this point the testimony of one of the three
brothers Huey so heartily disliked might well shed some light.

Some days after the fallen leader's funeral, and while the
legislature was still in session, a number of the Long satraps
were gathered in Governor Allen's office, lamenting the confusion into which a virtually leaderless assembly (in the sense
of having too many leaders) had fallen.

The leitmotiv of the parley held that things weren't like
that in the good old days when the Kingfish was around to
issue orders and see to it that they were carried out. The conversation finally veered to what a remarkable thing it was for

a little bit of an old town like Winnfield to have produced a superman like ol' Huey, especially when you realized it had never given to the world anyone else of comparable stature.

Earl Long, himself one of the thus disprized other products of Winnfield, listened in morose silence for a time to these observations. Finally he got up, moved to the door, paused, and said:

"You folks are right, of course. Huey was the only smart one from Winnfield. No manner of doubt about it." He scratched his chin meditatively and then added: "But I'm still here!"

On the other hand, those who casually dismiss Long as a conscienceless political gangster overlook the number of respects in which he was far, far ahead of his time. It is only since the mid-century's turn, for example, that clamor has become general to provide special advanced training for school children with well-above-normal mentality. Long proposed a program of this sort for Louisiana State University in his last broadcast, delivered two nights before he was shot. One of his last rational statements, expressed only moments before he lapsed into the drugged stupor from which he never really returned to consciousness, was a lament that he would be unable to carry out this project.

He enormously increased Louisiana's public debt with what proved to be a remarkably sound system of funding dedicated revenues into bonds, in order to give the state a highway network geared to the impending expansion of motorized traffic. In the 1960s the federal government followed the same line by laying out and constructing a vast system of interstate superhighways.

Almost without formal education himself—he never finished high school—he was like one possessed in his determination to put schooling within the reach of all by providing free textbooks, free transportation, free lunches, and the like. The medical school he founded at Louisiana State University, as though merely to spite Tulane for not conferring upon him at least one honorary degree, has won a recognized place as a great center of research and instruction; it fills what admittedly became a genuine need . . . and while today's income and inheritance levies do not set arbitrary limits like those proposed by Long in the early 1930s, the underlying principle of decentralization of wealth by heavy upper-bracket taxes is basically what he advocated.

None of this mitigates the heritage of corruption in public life that he bequeathed to Louisiana, or his ruthlessness, vindictiveness, and other reprehensible qualities. But he was very far from being merely another gangster.

The fact that the sons of both men whose lives ended so abruptly in September 1935 followed brilliantly in their fathers' footsteps may well be part of this same pattern of paradox.

Russell Long, only sixteen at the time of his father's death, enlisted in the Navy as a seaman during World War II, serving with distinction in the invasions of Africa, Sicily, and Italy (at Anzio), and advancing through promotion until he was a lieutenant at the time of his demobilization in 1945. In the election of January 1948 he supported the successful gubernatorial race of his uncle, Earl K. Long. In September of that same year, when Senator John H. Overton died with two years of his term yet to run, Governor Long supported his nephew for election to the vacancy.

He barely won by the slimmest sort of majority. The city of New Orleans cast a majority of twenty-five thousand votes against him. But he received much more ponderable support when he ran for the full Senate term two years later, and a more impressive vote still when he was re-elected in 1956. Finally, he was swept back into office in 1962 by a veritable landslide, receiving some 84 per cent of the votes cast.

In part this was a response to his generally independent stand on both local and national issues. In 1952, for example, he supported one of his father's uncompromising opponents, T. Hale Boggs, for governor against the candidate backed by his uncle Earl, then nearing the end of his first term as governor. But four years later he vigorously supported Earl against Mayor deLesseps Morrison of New Orleans when the latter made the first of two unsuccessful races for the governorship.

Beyond doubt, at least part of Russell's steadily growing strength was also due to the unmistakable fashion in which he proved himself an exceptionally able member of the Senate, being one of the first ranking figures in United States officialdom to recognize in Castro's rise to power a sinister portent, and to advocate immediate revision by this country of the sugar quota to counter the *Fidelista* drive toward Communist affiliation.

Following his sweeping victory in the late summer of 1962, he issued a modest victory statement in which he said in part:

"The most striking feature of my [re-election] was the majority recorded for me in New Orleans. In some of the wards where I had been defeated by a margin of seven to one fourteen years ago I was given a majority of as much as six to one. This could never have happened without a lot of people casting their first vote for a man who bears my family name. . . . I shall always appreciate those tolerant and generous persons who have seen fit to endorse me as the first member of my family to enjoy their support."

Dr. Carl Austin Weiss III, who was but three months old at the time of his father's death, was taken to New York by his mother when she left Louisiana to make her home in the

East. He was graduated from Columbia in 1958, and set out to make general surgery his field of medical practice. He was a full-time resident at St. Vincent's hospital for two years, but in July 1961 decided to specialize in orthopedic surgery, and entered the same hospital—Bellevue—where his father had been chief of clinic thirty years before.

He was married in 1961, and early in 1962 was called to active military service, being assigned as an air-force surgeon with the rank of captain to duty at Barksdale Field. This base is in Bossier parish, Louisiana, directly across the Red River from Shreveport, the city where Huey Long was married and where Russell Long was born. Thus the son of Carl Weiss was practicing medicine in Louisiana at the time the son of Huey Long won an overwhelming victory there in a campaign for the Senate seat formerly held by his father.

Long's presidential aspirations left his friend and secretary, Earle Christenberry an embarrassing $28,000 debt to pay.

"It is my firm belief now, and was my belief then," Christenberry asserts, "that Huey would not have been a candidate for president himself prior to 1940. He told me in 1935 that he intended to stump the country, sounding out sentiment before deciding whom he would support *against* Roosevelt.

"To that end he had me purchase from Graybar one sound truck which was the last word in mobile loud-speaker installations. It came in a day or two before his death, and I sweated it out for many a month, raising some $28,000 to pay for it. Graybar looked to me for payment because I had placed the order. My recollection is that the money was not forthcoming until late in the Leche campaign, for I would not let them use the truck until it was paid for."

In retrospect, two predictions about Huey Long hold a certain interest. One, by Elmer Irey, is merely academic, since it deals with what *would* have happened. In closing his chapter on "The Gentleman from Louisiana" Mr. Irey notes that to him the "important thing about the Huey Long gang's downfall" is the following:

"I hope this story will destroy for all time one of the blackest libels ever made against the American system of democracy. This libel states that had not Dr. Weiss (or somebody) assassinated Huey Long, our country might well have been taken over by the Kingfish as dictator. The inference is clear. Our country was no match for Huey's genius and ruthlessness.

"I would suggest that the bullet that killed Huey . . . merely saved Huey from going to jail. . . . Huey had broken the law and was to be indicted for it when he was killed."

When evaluating this forecast, the first thought that comes to mind is a matter of record: within a month of Long's death one of his top-echelon supporters was brought to trial on a tax-evasion indictment. Mr. Irey's organization had selected this particular indictment because it was regarded as the government's strongest case against any Long administration official. At the trial's close the jury verdict was "not guilty"!

In the light of past experience the conjecture that Long would in time have gained the presidency is not one casually to be shrugged aside. Had he ever attained "My First Days in the White House," subjection of the large cities (not the rural areas) would have been his primary objective. Just as New Orleans was the last foothold of the carpetbaggers in the 1870s, Boston, New York, Cleveland, Philadelphia, Chicago, and others might have learned what it is like to live under the rule of force from without.

The other prediction referred to above was made by Mason Spencer in the course of a bitter address on the floor of the House of Representatives in April 1935. Spencer withdrew from public office at the close of this legislative term, as did also Dr. Octave Pavy. Both died of heart attacks within weeks of one another in the summer of 1962. But whereas Spencer forsook politics almost altogether, Dr. Pavy retained a very active quasi-Warwickian interest in parochial campaigns.

He retired from forty years of the practice of medicine at an advanced age, and moved from his home at Leonville on Bayou Teche to Opelousas. But his popularity along the bayou-side, where by that time he had delivered more than fifty-eight hundred babies, was so widespread that patients demanded he continue to treat them, so that he had to establish a small office. From this GHQ he successfully brought about the defeat of an opposition sheriff, winning a scandalously large sum of money in bets on the outcome of the election. He converted most of his winnings into currency, packed them into an ordinary water-bucket, and carrying this, he marched triumphantly around and around the Opelousas courthouse square, shouting his exultation to the four winds.

He had been among the first to cheer Mason Spencer's closing remarks in April 1935 at a special session during which the Kingfish brought about the enactment of a bill which to all intents and purposes gave him the sole right to appoint every commissioner and other polling-booth official in every voting precinct for every election throughout Louisiana.

"I am not one of those who cries 'Hail, Caesar!'" Spencer said in slow and measured tones, "nor have I cried 'Jail Caesar!' But this ugly bill disfranchises the white people of Louisiana. . . . I can see blood on the marble floor of this capitol, for if you ride this thing through, it will travel with the white horse of death. In the pitiful story of Esau the Bible teaches us it is possible for a man to sell his own birthright. But the gravestones on a thousand battlefields teach you that you cannot sell the birthright of another white man!"

Within five months there was blood on the marble floor of the capitol.

DATE DUE

NOV 1 9 '63			
DEC 1 0 '63			
MAR 9 '64			
MAR 1 8 '64			
JUN 17 '65			
APR 1 0 '67			
APR 2 5 '67			
MAY 9 '67			
FEB 18 '72			
DEC 1 '73			
AP 12 77			
GAYLORD			PRINTED IN U.S.A.